591.5 Cosgrove, Margaret.
C
    Animals alone and
    together, their
    solitary and social
    lives

DATE		
MAR 4		
NOV 24		
OCT 26		
NOV 9		
APR 11		

ANIMALS ALONE AND TOGETHER

Their Solitary and Social Lives

ANIMALS ALONE AND TOGETHER

Their Solitary and Social Lives

Written and illustrated by
Margaret Cosgrove

DODD, MEAD & COMPANY NEW YORK

1   2   3   4   5   6   7   8   9   10

Library of Congress Cataloging in Publication Data

Cosgrove, Margaret.
Animals alone and together, their solitary
and social lives.

Bibliography: p.
Includes index.
SUMMARY: Examines the principal groupings in which
animals live, the reasons for these divisions, and the
behavior of animals in them.
1.   Animals, Habits and behavior of—Juvenile litera-
ture.   2.   Social behavior in animals—Juvenile litera-
ture.   [1.   Animals—Habits and behavior]   I.   Title.
QL751.5.C65   591.5   77-12625
ISBN 0-396-07520-7

Contents

	Introduction: To Be Alone or Not to Be	7
1.	Seeking Each Other	9
2.	Forces That Push and Pull	19
3.	Three Keys to Coexistence	31
4.	Bird Biographies	41
5.	A Word About Fighting	53
6.	A Word About Killing	57
7.	Hunters and Hunteds	63
8.	The Great and Powerful	84
9.	Our Nearest Relatives	90
10.	The Unsociables	101
11.	Some Practically Perfect Societies	110
	Epilogue: A Word About Human Beings	119
	Suggested Reading	121
	Index	123

Introduction: To Be Alone
or Not to Be

PEOPLE SEEK each other. A very few dwell like hermits, wishing to be let alone as much as possible. Others have just a few acquaintances. The lives of many are bound up mostly with their own family, and still others prefer to be in crowds. Most human beings desire solitude occasionally, but often enough enjoy the company of friends, and this is probably the happiest way to be.

Animals also have many different lifestyles in respect to alone or together-living. Some are joiners, some are not. There are flocks of birds, herds of elk, schools of fish. We hear of packs of wolves, prides of lions. A lone horse in a field will hasten over to a fence to nuzzle another at the first opportunity, and a dog goes all out of its mind with joy at the return of its master. But whoever heard of a pack of bears, or for that matter a herd of porcupines? Animals such as these seem to live out their lives quite alone.

Animals, then, are solitary or social, or somewhere in between. We catch glimpses of their lives—a whale surfaces and blows, then disappears from view again in the mysterious depths of the ocean. A troop of monkeys chatters noisily in tropical treetops and then becomes as silent as if it had totally vanished. A wasp appears from nowhere, poises in midair a few moments, then darts away to nowhere. Fragments of lives that can be pieced together to form

7

a patchwork quilt for each kind of animal that exists. We note only bits of the design at a time.

And so we wonder why alone, why together, for animals? Why do some avoid or even violently repel another, when others are attracted to members of their species, never liking to be solitary? Why do some shun others at one time but are drawn to them another, and when do they act in harmony or hostility toward each other? It is not simply a matter of the beasts eating, fighting, and mating, as many people believe; their lives are much more complex than that. To get along, to survive, all must recognize friend or enemy, and send and receive messages in communication with them. There must be countless signs, signals, and ceremonies which convey feeling and intentions.

Though animals of different kinds sometimes associate with each other, we will delve mostly into the ways of animals with just their own species here. Two great aspects of their lives will be under investigation: how they relate to each other, or do not, and how their way of life benefits them—or does not. Neither animal nor human being can be a complete Robinson Crusoe all his life. In the difference between going it alone or in the company of others, there lies many a story.

1. Seeking Each Other

OF ALL THE thousands of animal species which exist, few roam aimlessly through woods or field, sky or water. The lives, activities, and whereabouts of most are an orderly sort of business. For whatever each does there is some explanation, whether or not we know what it is. As each animal fits into its own living pattern, it

> relates to its own species,
>
> relates to other species around it, and
>
> relates to its environment

in precise ways. There are reasons and seasons for all its behavior.

A society is not just a collection of individuals, like a crowd gathered in a train station, or clustered around a drinking fountain on a hot day. An assortment of human strangers may congregate in a room for the purpose of forming a club for some mutual interest. At first, many of the gatherers are cautious, or hesitant, as they begin to feel each other out and relate to each other. Friendships are made, even a few dislikes may be formed. After a while a president and officers are elected, committees are appointed. As time goes on, relationships shift, strengthen, and change, like multicolored oil paints swirling through water.

A society is like a club; it is an organized gathering. Some structure, some rules and regulations, are necessary lest members pull all in different directions, individuals suffer for it, and the group

There is room for much variety within a social structure.

falls to pieces. "United we stand, divided we fall." The more one peers into a society's workings, the more meaningful patterns emerge.

Just as human social preferences are many and varied, so are those of animals. There are many kinds of apartness and togetherness. Keeping in mind that animals do not necessarily remain in one category all the time, let us examine the principal kinds of groupings.

Solitaries

To begin with, there are such examples as the bears that ramble through most of their lives alone, relating very little to others. Male and female spend a few fond weeks together at mating time, and then part. Mother and cubs form a close twosome or threesome until the cubs are grown enough to fend for themselves. A number of other single-living animals are so secretive that their lives are difficult to study.

Some animals live by themselves because they have left their groups or have seemed to become outcasts; we do not always know why. Most young male mammals especially, as soon as they can take care of themselves, leave home of their own accord or are driven away by their mother, or in some cases by the father or other adults. Certain animals live as hermits or nomads part of the year and are group members the rest of it.

Aggregations

Sometimes animals come together in bunches just because they happen to. Perhaps the best food is there, or there is security in huddling up, or for some other reason, such as moths and beetles collecting to zoom around a streetlamp, attracted by the light. Animals of many species gather at a water hole to drink. Frogs in spring are drawn to a swamp or pond to mate. Large aggregations of ladybird beetles ("ladybugs") hibernate in masses, squeezed in cracks of logs and crevices in a stone wall, and a tangle of snakes holds a little warmth among them as they wrap around each others' bodies in an underground hole in winter.

Animals in such bunches, or aggregations, do not relate to each other as group members as far as we can tell, other than to be

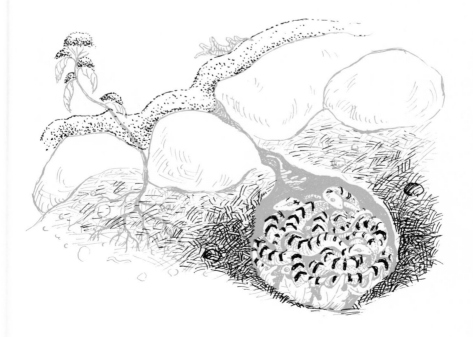

Roe deer family

aware of each others' presences. There are no leaders, there is no organization to the group; they are mostly just a simple collection of individuals in the same place at the same time.

FAMILIES

A mother bear has the raising of her cubs to do by herself. A father midwife toad carries his strings of eggs twisted around his legs until the tadpoles hatch. But sometimes both animal parents join in the rearing of the offspring, remaining faithful to each other for just the season, or in many cases for their entire lives. Bird parents are particularly famous for being loyal, dedicated parents who both share in the hard work of feeding, caring for, and teaching the birdlings.

Fox parents also raise their young together. After the cubs are nearly grown and have left home, these parents often separate (as it is easier for them to find food alone during the difficult winter months), but at least some pairs return to each other the following February or March. Coyotes of America and golden jackals of Africa form affectionate family groups, and at least some of these mate for life. A wolf male is a most devoted father, as we shall see. Some fishes by no means neglect their eggs and young, and the stickleback father fans his lake-bottom nest faithfully until the young emerge to swim away on their own.

A tiny, toylike antelope of Africa, the dik-dik, forms family units of the parents plus two or three fawns, slipping through the low, dark places of their forest always together. African wart

12

hogs also form two-parent families. Beaver mother and father build and live in their partly submerged lodge with two sets of young: the newest kits, and the older yearlings. The long-armed gibbon male and female, small apes of Southeast Asia, form a lasting, close relationship with each other, taking good care of their two or three little apes.

Just as the small, central unit of an atom is called the nucleus, this basic two-parent unit with offspring is known as the "nuclear" family.

Extended Families

Revolving around a human nuclear family, somewhat the way electrons revolve around in an atom, often are grandparents and cousins, aunts and uncles. Just so with some animals, where adult offspring, with or without young of their own, stay on together to form an extended family. This is true notably of wolves, where it is still possible for them to live in a natural state, and of some other canine species. It is also typical of monkeys and apes. Often there are "aunties," as with elephants, penguins, and many whales, who take part in looking after the young. A wolf pack may have "aunts" and "uncles" also, which may not mate themselves but share in caring for the cubs.

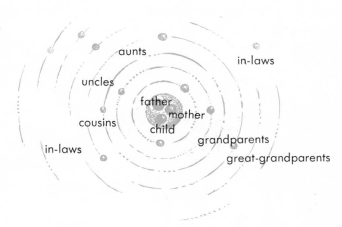

Young male wild mountain sheep

BACHELOR GROUPS

Young adult males, as was mentioned, leave their home situation usually to roam solitary as "bachelors" until they mate. These, as well as older males, often band together in groupings, small or large. There are stud groups of wild horses and zebras, also of whales, wild mountain sheep, gulls, and baboons. Sometimes only two or three form companionships and hunt together, as do some young lions, perhaps never settling down to join a pride.

HAREMS

A number of females lorded over by one male is called a harem. Some stay formed all year round, others for a short time only. Such an arrangement brings up many questions we will explore. Why do some males merit the possession of many females, and why do these accept such a system? Is this because there are fewer males, or not? How do harem wives get along together under such conditions?

Harem of pronghorns

MATRIARCHIES

But there are many groups, even very large ones, composed entirely of females and young. Or there may be mixed groups of both sexes, plus the offspring, with a female as a sometime-leader. Such a head is a matriarch (Latin *mater*, "mother"), though there may be several to a group. Bees and elephants, for example, form matriarchies. Of course there are also groups of other kinds with strong male leadership.

TROOPS

A troop generally refers to a group of monkeys or apes, though such a social structure may take any of several forms. It can be a two-parent family, as with gibbons, but is often more of an extended family or several of them. It may be harems united in a larger body or even a loose, open arrangement of visiting relatives who come to call, stay a while, and then leave.

15

A seal colony

COLONIES

A colony often denotes a large group of creatures living in some far-flung outpost, as the early American colonies settled in a remote area from where their originators came from. Huge numbers of penguins dwelling together in parts of the Antarctic continent form colonies, as do other sea birds such as gannets and gulls, nesting densely on isolated cliffs or islands. Certain other birds, however, colonize in treetops. Huge numbers of seals land annually on islands or beaches to form breeding colonies.

But there are also fascinating colonies of quite another sort, formed of very small, backboneless water animals, usually of the seas rather than fresh water. Plantlike growths cling to rocks and wharf posts and small, lacy mats grow on shells and some crabs' backs. Each such grouping is composed of many tiny animals adjoined, never faring forth alone once they have settled down. Corals living on sea bottoms are communal also. Their dried, delicate skeletons can be purchased for admiration and study. A separate, flower-like organism related to jellyfish once dwelt in each tiny hole. Stony corals secrete the lime (calcium) and thus form islands and the tremendous reefs on which ships can go aground.

MIGRATIONS

It happens each year, in spring and fall in temperate climates, that great numbers of animals gather to travel to other places. This

is mainly for the purpose of finding food when cold weather descends, and later returning to breeding grounds. Birds, of course, are the prime migrants, often winging on incredible journeys of thousands of miles. Wild bighorn sheep of America's West migrate from high mountain pastures to lower ones, and vast herds of caribou move across the frozen reaches of northern Canada, Scandinavia, and Russia. Even some butterflies, such as the handsome black and orange monarch and the lovely painted lady, flutter great distances. Locusts and lemmings are famous for their periodic surges by the millions across the land. Many seals, whales, and fishes also migrate.

What goes on within these groups we do not entirely know. At one end of the scale, the butterflies probably interrelate very little among the travelers. Among more complex organisms different degrees of relationships occur within such groups as the hoofed mammals. But for the most part, all are simply moved and unified by the same compelling cause. But cooperation is visible, for example, among wild geese, which usually travel as extended families or groups of families. Here temporary leaders are relieved by others as they retreat to the rear of the line, and members exchange places from one side to the other of their famous V-shaped formation. Such interchange alters airflow stresses on their wings, as each is affected by the currents from the aeronaut in front, and relative positions are important. The constant communion of their honking, helping to keep them in contact, drifts down to the awestruck observer.

Wart hog family

2. *Forces That Push and Pull*

ONE ATTRACTION that drew animals together to live in groups, particularly birds and mammals, was long held to be a sort of social instinct that held them in pack or herd. But why, then, were not the bear, leopard, and other loners subject to this? Clearly there were other reasons to be sought than some vague instinct.

Another reason was held to be sex. Being "just beasts," were not animals constantly interested in mating or just sniffing around each other? This explanation seemed obvious.

But regarding this, some surprising facts have been upturned in the last few decades. The first one points out that males and females of most species live separately from each other much of the time. The second finds that the egg, or ovum, within mature human females can become ready to be fertilized throughout the year, and the third reveals that in the majority of other animals it does not. Most species have a season for breeding, sometimes a very short one of less than a day, very often only once annually. Mice, rabbits, and a few other mammals may produce several litters per year. Many mammals, fish, and lizards are timed to produce their offspring only in spring (in temperate zones), as the young require all the summer they can get in which to gain strength to face the hardships of winter. Birds have one brood, sometimes two, each summer.

But a mother gorilla produces a single infant once every three or four years, and a full-grown male gorilla may procreate as little as once a year. The cow elephant becomes pregnant only every two or three years, and as rarely as every eight or nine years when living conditions are poor. The bull elephant, though mature around his twelfth or thirteenth birthday, often cannot win himself a chance to mate until an entire decade after that.

These animals live in societies with little inclination to mate much, or most, of the time. Others roam nomad-like or in separate male or female groups with impulses only to steer clear of the opposite sex, and the truly solitary avoid their own sex as well. But as surely as a magnet draws a compass needle, female and male throughout the world are drawn together when their time comes, in a magnificent pageant of diverse and fascinating behavior.

When animals are not in mating mood, they are more or less just animals, sort of unisex creatures. Some may nevertheless stay with their mate for some time, or depart from him or her and live each in its own way. But all are directed by strong forces which cause them to come together to dwell socially, or to repel others and live in solitude. So ethologists (who study the natural behavior of animals) have discovered that there are a number of fundamental urges that pull animals together or push them apart from each other. Probably the most powerful is the need for food.

To Eat—

Just how each animal fulfills its nutrition needs is the largest determining factor in its way of life. Consider a bear. It eats an extremely varied diet: berries, grasses, nuts, certain roots, dead creatures (carrion), eggs, garbage, fish, ants, beetles, grasshoppers and honey when it can get any of these; also, to a lesser extent, woodchucks, frogs, mice, and a very occasional stray lamb or fawn. (A bear is an omnivore, an eater of both plants and animals.) It plainly needs much food to sustain its big body. Therefore it would seem to require a wide span of countryside in order to stay in business. A herd of bears would find it impossible for all to find enough food in a given area unless it were unnaturally plentiful, and so they shun each other, trying to keep distances between them.

Or let us take a look at wild bighorn sheep of America's western regions. They graze in herds, spread out over mountain slopes, moving on to new high pastures as they nibble up their present food sources, which will grow again. One or another will spot a new, fresher growth and the rest will follow, and there is enough to go around.

A wolf or eagle is still another story. Each of these predators, or hunting animals, catches its prey usually only one try out of several, often making many frustrating attempts before succeeding, sometimes going several days without a sizable meal. But these carnivores (flesh-eaters) find each such meal all in a bundle, so to speak, which is one other animal. The herbivores, or plant-eaters, find their food spread out around them. Some graze on the grass and herbs of fields and prairies or pluck fruit from trees. Some browse on foliage, others paw under snow for moss and lichens. One luncheon for the wolf or eagle is a single package, equal to the steady chomping on grass, fruit, and mushrooms that the herbivore turns into flesh, which may be consumed by the carnivore. As one animal may thus be the food of another, there is a delicate balance between the ways of diner and dinner.

—or Be Eaten

Safety is just about as important as eating, for it does an animal no good to dwell in a land of plenty if it is going to be someone else's food. Though the hunting animal is very capable of fear, and can itself be sought after, the chief threat to many is only man, whereas the grazing animal has more natural enemies to be afraid of. How far will an animal, frightened, threatened, and at the same time hungry, venture to find sustenance at the risk of its life? Neither prey nor predator can win or lose every encounter. It all comes down to an almost mathematical equation of how well-nourished an animal can maintain itself at the least risk, with many factors involved. Each one pits its unique means of defense against other animals' means of overcoming it. There are even ways to defeat a porcupine. Its formidable quills, the gazelle's or leopard's speed, the skunk's scent—there is no end to the weapons of defense employed. But use of these is also intertwined with the aloneness or togetherness of the bearers of them.

The bear, needing to scour the countryside for its menu, can afford to live alone, defending itself with its size. Most grizzly, black, and polar bears, however, are much more likely to run or hide than to pick a fight, unless surprised or cornered. The wolf and eagle, being good hunters, are good fighters, but still neither asks for trouble. The wolf, victim of much untrue publicity about its evil ways, will flee in practically all circumstances except self-defense, and of course food-getting, when the odds are in favor of it. Wild adult wolves, placed experimentally in large enclosures with a man seated in a corner quietly reading a book, have shown extreme fear and panic reactions, trying to escape by scaling the high fence or tunneling beneath it. The most fearsome predators rarely go around simply attacking without reason.

nutrition in one piece

food all spread out

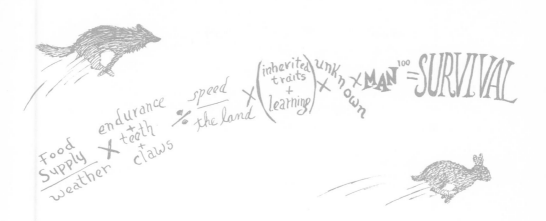

$$\frac{Food\ Supply}{weather} \times \frac{endurance + teeth + claws}{teeth} \times \frac{speed}{\%\ the\ land} \times \binom{inherited\ traits + learning}{} \times unknown \times MAN^{100} = SURVIVAL$$

The plant-eaters are poor fighters generally, but swift of foot or hoof. Lesser ones are usually creatures of the dark, dwelling singly. But bigger ones graze in herds, small or large, and we wonder how this works for or against them. On one hand, a predator is less likely to charge into a group of animals than to attack one alone. We will see how these hunters try to cut the weaker and slower out of a herd. On the other hand, animals in a group are more conspicuous, less able to hide. They must counteract their visibility in some way, as by all members being attentive for the faintest suspicious sound, scent, or movement from any direction. (Baboons are daytime feeders, which makes them all the more visible; they could feed at night, but then their predators would be harder to spot also!) Daytime, or diurnal, eaters that sleep nights on the open ground, as zebras do, must still never let their guard down. There is always at least one wakeful member which stands alert while others are sleeping.

A whole school of fish that could vanish down the maw of a pursuer will scatter, each silvery individual darting like lightning in a different direction, and few can be caught. But some birds react in opposite fashion. A flock of starlings in flight tightens its formation, and the bird of prey in pursuit does not dare risk injuring itself seriously by flying into their midst. There are the many alarm signals that exist also. Antelopes and rabbits, for example, will recognize the stiffened, taller posture of another species member which spots possible danger lurking, and all heads turn toward the suspected threat. Birds utter alarm sounds, often understood by birds of all species within hearing, and mammals as well. Food and safety are urgent needs of the present.

There are also basic needs that affect the future of animals' survival that draw them together.

To Mate—

The animal which lives in the most alone way possible must drop its behavior of avoidance at intervals if its race is to continue. Obviously, two solitaries of opposite sex must come together to reproduce. Some animals such as insects, frogs, and snakes meet, mate, and part, and in few cases does either parent have much to do with care of the offspring once the eggs are laid. Let us contrast these to the warm-blooded feather and fur bearers, the mammals.

It is more true of nonhuman animals than of people that "In the spring a young man's fancy turns to thoughts of love," as the old saying claims. Actually a young man's fancy may turn in that direction any time of year, but male animals get romantic notions less often. Certain males caged with a female at other times than

The very visible little prairie dog fits its environment by living in protective groups.

their breeding season may attack and even kill her, so strong is their urge to be alone or with other males most of the year. Bodies must be prepared, inside and out, for their important act of procreation. The ovum within the female must be exactly ready to receive a sperm from the male which will develop into an embryo, or new creature. As we say of our pet dog or cat female at this time, she is "in heat" (or in estrus). This generally determines the response of male and female toward each other. His body must be ready and waiting whenever the shorter period of her readiness arrives.

The whole romance may be short—quickly begun and soon over. But in very many animals it takes a longer time, ranging from a simple to a very elaborate affair. It often begins with a courtship which can be long and complicated.

There is a whole rainbow of variations on these matters among the multitudes of animal species. On the paler side is the bear, who spends little effort making up to his chosen one, though these partners may spend several weeks roaming together, apparently fondly, before and after the actual act of mating. (On the dullest side is really the domestic dog, who wastes little time or ceremony either way.) On the most colorful end of the spectrum are the birds. Many engage in extraordinary behavior, some wearing spectacular plumage, others with riots of song and/or performances. In between are the hoofed mammals, where many of the males grow powerful antlers or sport splendid horns which they brandish ferociously. It seems to be necessary in courting by cats to be rough and noisy. All the show and activity of courtship serve several important functions, in bringing a couple together in a state of excitement, eliminating competitors, and establishing a pair bond of short or long duration, and of course effectuating the act of mating. Even porcupines manage.

There are obstacles to be overcome. Two individuals must find a member of the opposite sex (locating each other can be difficult with the live-alones) and determine its body readiness for mating.

Pair bond, beavers

If she (it is more often she) is indifferent to begin with, her interest can be aroused. There is the necessity by the male to let it be known that he is very much a male, and other males please do not interfere with what he regards as his, whether this is a female, or several of them, or the land he occupies. Other males will be ousted from the area.

An antelope, the Uganda kob, holds forth on African plains in dramatic fashion. Of many hundreds, only a few males will breed each new generation. Spaced out across a sort of permanent tournament field, each of these has fought for and now possesses his own plot, which he must continue to hold onto against all challengers if he can, or else leave this very serious game and join the non-breeding bachelors beyond the sidelines. It is to these land-holding champions that the females come, and though the males strike handsome poses, arching their necks far backward with noses pointed skyward and strutting with small, dainty steps as if in a courtly dance, it is as much their position on prime land as their impressiveness that draws the females. Center locations are most desirable. As an example nearer home, the sage grouse on their Wyoming strutting grounds produce extravagant theatrical performances that rival the Uganda kobs'. Sage hens, attracted to the cocks in their stately, sometimes wild ballet by which they strive to win the most sought-after mating grounds, usually breed with only the few males that are best-landed.

Pair bond, Canada geese

Animals are prevented from attacking in many instances by turn-off signs made by another. In spring a male American robin will fly at another male that trespasses on his territory, the red breast of the intruder a bright flag that triggers the first into fighting with another of his own species. But the female's paler front, plus her postures, advise him that she is not a contender for his property, and she thus turns off, or inhibits, his aggressiveness. And so through songs and signs, injury is averted bloodlessly. The young would never get hatched and raised if all disagreements were simply battled out.

It is the female animal that has the last word, for the male rarely forces her into mating. Her unwillingness to cooperate indicates that the ovum is unready. Rape is very scarce among the "lower" animals. The ceremonies, the bright colors and dances of many birds, the antics of hoofed animals and varied behavior of others, all serve their function in the awakening of affection and preparing the way toward the climax of the union.

—AND RAISE THE YOUNG ONES

A bear mother teaches her exuberant cubs to stop playing and go climb a tree or head for cover when she gives a danger signal. An eaglet or a bobcat kitten is taught how to dismember a mouse delivered to it. A reluctant little sea otter has to be taught how to swim.

27

Mother-young bond

There is a great deal that bird and mammal offspring have to learn. The task of teaching them most often falls to the mother, though most bird and some mammal fathers also share the responsibility. In certain mammal groups all adults join in bringing food to the young, protecting them, and offering them affection. In still other societies there are "baby sitters" or the "aunties"—other adults, female or occasionally male, who watch over a whole nursery. Among many monkeys and apes, older brothers and sisters measure their abilities to the needs of the little ones in assisting in their care. In some groups a mother will adopt orphans or nurse any youngster, though in others they do not.

The young wild animal that is found and brought into a human home may be doomed, since the human being cannot teach it what it needs to know. Grown into an adult, not suited to continue living in a house, or unhappy when caged, leashed, or restricted from its own environment and kind, its chances of survival are often poor when it is turned loose again.

The road to maturity may be bumpy and long, but it is the only way for a young animal to get where it needs to go. Skill must be developed in the use of its weapons and tools: claws, teeth, and muscles. Even a little elephant has to learn how to keep from stumbling over its trunk, and how to pick a leaf. There are feelings about weather and directions to be acquired, about paths, boundaries, and landmarks, and there are places of food and water to be remembered. There are the signs of lurking danger to become sensitized to and translated into understanding.

The young animal must learn the customs of its species, and ways of communicating them. Whom are you allowed to tease without getting into trouble, and whom had you better not? How do you get along with some stern old leader or with mischief-makers? To whom and how do you offer your respect? How do you read signs in your fellows: the bristling of hair, the angle at which a tail is held, and what does a slightly opened mouth mean? The young animal needs to be protected while it experiments, watches, mimics, and makes its own mistakes.

A LAST COMPELLING PULL

We have seen some good, practical reasons for animals to live in smoothly running social groups. There are other, less obvious ones, which are not yet understood well. We do know that animals

REASONS
FOR
GROUP
LIVING

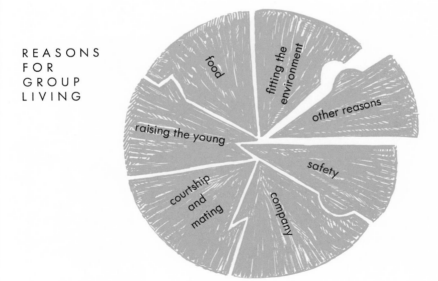

29

are often stimulated to do things because they see others do them, such as drinking or eating, which could result in greater safety or health. An antelope or baboon, for example, had better drink, thirsty or not, while its group is at the water hole, for if it leaves them to drink later it may be pounced upon. We know also that many animals must follow their deeply inborn inclinations about mating, in regard to solitary or social habits. This is one reason why some species in zoos seldom or never breed, as they need their natural conditions around them for psychological reasons.

Lone-livers have their built-in mechanisms for keeping distances from one another. But at least some of them, if trained from earliest days, do not develop ways of preferring solitude when there is little need for it, but seem to enjoy companionship. And so we see that there is one last, powerful pull in animals seeking each other—the need for company. Something deep inside probably even the most solitary can hear a mysterious call of comfort in nearness to others.

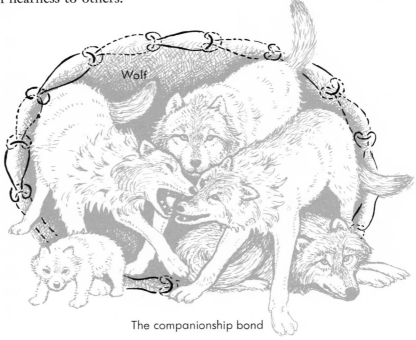

Wolf

The companionship bond

3. *Three Keys to Coexistence*

WHAT KEEPS a lone-living puma at a distance from every other puma, seldom treading too close to its den or hunting grounds? When two lizards want the same food, space, or mate, how is it decided who gets which—or do they fight it out savagely? How is an argument in a troop of gorillas settled?

To find out how animals cope with each other, we need to find well-fitting keys to unlock some mysteries of animal coexistence. Amidst all the hazards of living and stress of relationships they could not be expected to think out or plan their courses of action as human beings can better do for themselves. In the immensely complicated journeys of their lives, the best computer could not flash out directives on how each unique creature should meet the myriad problems of surviving.

For a young animal preparing to deal with challenges of its world, a time of dependency is necessary while it traverses the route to maturity. This is what childhood is about. Birds have longer "childhoods" than do insects and reptiles; most mammals have longer ones still. The keys to getting along with other animals are acquired by the closely interwoven ways: instinct and learning.

The young animal is born already equipped with certain automatic ways it will react that it has never been taught. It hatched or was born with mechanisms that directed some of its behavior.

31

The newborn fawn flattens itself to the ground at a signal from its mother and will stir not a hair. The just-hatched little turtle "knows" which way to waddle toward water at once. A mother bird does not have to be taught how to construct the typical, intricate nest of her species, and certain father fish, such as the little stickleback, instinctively build theirs.

Such mechanical actions each animal inherits from its ancestors. These inborn, or innate, habits come forth when they are triggered by internal states of the body and by external conditions. Some show up very early; some do not appear until later in life. And so a bird nearing maturity, never having been there before, has an innate chain reaction set off in him by (a) the growing readiness of his brain, glands, and other organs, and (b) environmental cues, such as the precise length of the day's sunlight. These guide, say, most songbirds into locating and laying claim to a homesite, obtaining a mate, declaring publicly through singing his right to both, helping build a nest, and fertilizing and taking his turn incubating his mate's eggs.

Learning is the other way of preparing the young for independent living. It is more easily controlled than instinct, which is programmed into brain and body cells. Experiences give pleasant or unpleasant consequences. The coyote cub learns what to eat by nuzzling its snout against the muzzle of either parent as he or she eats, and it learns what not to eat by becoming sick or hurt through unwise tries. This is trial-and-error learning—the cub tried something that didn't work. The grizzly bear mother must teach her cub much of its sense of fear, for its own good. Animals learn by copying or mimicking what they see others do. A newborn monkey clings to its mother's fur purely by instinct, but its mother is a better parent with her second baby, from watching others with

Instinct

and

learning

theirs, and by having received a good mothering herself; she has learned from these experiences.

It is often hard to tell whether instinct or learning exerts the most influence over behavior. A puma mother sometimes takes just one kitten at a time with her to patiently demonstrate hunting skills, giving it practice exercises, building on its stalking and pouncing instincts. Together the cubs might have been too fun-loving to have gotten much out of a class lesson.

What of different species together? One scientist asked himself whether aggressiveness between natural enemies was inherited or learned. Dr. Z. Y. Kuo raised kittens (of house cats) from birth with baby rats. On reaching adulthood, a small number of the cats hunted rats; their innate behavior came through strongly enough to impel them to do so even without training. A larger number never chased rats at all, as they had never been taught.

Through the intermingling of the two tools of instinct and learning, animals grow up to fit into their place in the wild. Now on to three keys to understanding behavior which help them live with a minimum of strife.

SPACED OUT

It is a lucky person who has a room all his own, or even a part of a room everyone respects. People can retreat into houses or apartments, leaving the outside world behind, for "a man's home is his castle." From hide-and-seek through many another game the cry of triumph and relief is "Home free!"

It is a basic need in most living creatures to have some sort of space around them. The majority of animals have a sense of locality, sometimes a very strong one. Human hunters have taken advantage of this by chasing some, such as the beautiful pronghorn antelope of western states, around and around their land area, knowing that they were unable to cease clinging to it when they might have escaped—but into a great, unfamiliar world.

Every animal needs a private space.

The area might be small, sometimes just a nest or den. It might be large, a huge home range about which the animal roams for food. A mother black bear with cubs will stay within about 300 square miles (twenty miles across). Bullfrogs and crocodiles, wasps and dragonflies patrol their territories. Animals such as orangutans and deer share their wild homes with others of their kind, but mockingbirds will not tolerate other mockingbirds than their own mates on their land. Such birds and mammals with a strong sense of territory will defend their area, with fighting if necessary, from trespassers of their own species. Hyenas are noted for this, as are wolves. Many lizards go through vivid color changes and/or

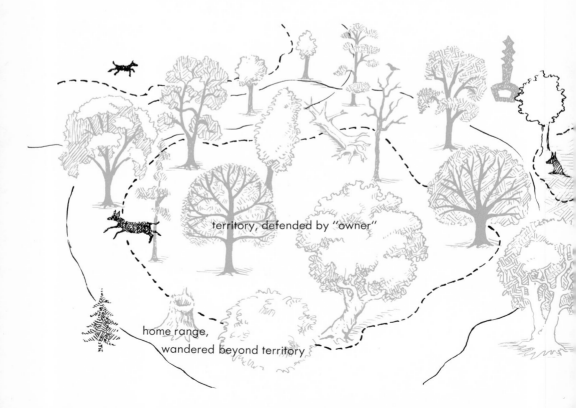

territory, defended by "owner"

home range,
wandered beyond territory

assume postures that warn intruders away. Even fiddler crabs on the beach have their own patches of sand. Territories have more or less definite boundaries, though some overlap.

There are systems of posting them against invaders which others understand. Some kinds of hippopotamus spray urine and dung backwards on bushes and tall grass, fanning them about with their tails. A buck rabbit marks brush and upright sticks by rubbing glands under his chin against them, leaving a scent. Glands under the tails of beavers also leave scent on the sometimes high pats they pile up, and woodchucks, foxes, and rabbits also deposit scent on their droppings meant to mark locations. Human beings build fences and walls or grow hedges around their yards, and some city dwellers have four locks on their doors!

It is usually not necessary to defend these territories by hard fighting, as they are respected. Animals of the same species may cross them at times but are not likely to occupy them, as is the case with pumas. Even though the owner may be weaker or smaller, he is most likely to win a dispute, even against a regiment of intruders bent on taking over.

Whether an animal roams freely within a vague home range, or will fight desperately to hang onto his territory, or does neither, most have a deep need for breathing room, a kind of fortress of air, around it, which confers a feeling of safety. Many have their own flight distance, which is an almost exact, though variable, space it maintains around it—if an intruder enters this the first one will flee. Deer of all kinds, which includes moose and elk, do not do well in crowded pens, as closeness is much to the discomfort of wild hoofed animals. Just as some people can feel deeply distressed by confinement in an elevator or crowd, wild animals have an even more natural, innate need for "elbow room," an individual, private space out of touching distance, which means security and life to them. Snarling, hissing, or actual attack by one may be its response to a vital threat it feels when its invisible fence has been crashed through.

The bear that lives by itself is its own boss. Animals in a group can exist seldom, if ever, in purest democracy, all being exactly equal. Someone must have first chance, second, and third at food and other necessities when these are limited, as they often are. Some with more intelligence, strength, or a positiveness of attitude must have the authority to keep peace or take command. Thus it works out best in many groups that there be some order of importance among members which helps avoid quarreling, conflict, and bloodshed. These require energy which animals often cannot afford to waste; fighting can result in injuries or deaths that can harm or even destroy the whole group. When a few gorillas, usually a peaceful lot, fall to quibbling among themselves, the big male leader merely turns a fearsome look upon them from beneath his heavy brow, and peace descends.

And so, just as farmers observed long ago in barnyard chickens, most groups develop some system of levels among members. One, sometimes several, hold highest rank or dominance, grading down

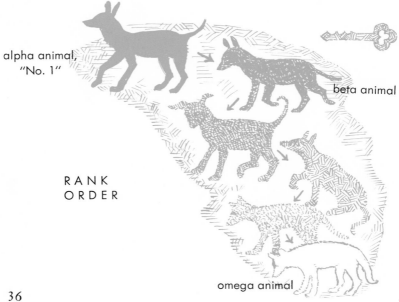

alpha animal,
"No. 1"

beta animal

RANK
ORDER

omega animal

step by step to the least powerful ones of all. This order can be observed, for example, in schoolyards at times, where there are those who are always game leaders, those who are followers, scaling down some ladder of influence to the quietest and least athletic, who are last to be chosen.

This system in animals gives security, in that each member knows where he or she stands. The weak are sometimes protected by the stronger. African wild dogs have been seen looking after the old and sick, even seeing to it that injured pack members got food. This rank order (also called "pecking order") or dominance hierarchy, makes for more cooperation and success in group living than if each member did just as he or she pleased. It is sometimes hard to discern if a rank order actually exists or who the chief animal is, as he or she is usually no bully, and so harmoniously does the group operate.

Uniting the Parts: Communication

A sports hero or presidential candidate does not have to proclaim his opinion of himself in so many words—though he often does. Neither does a shy person or a sad or happy one often need to describe how he or she feels. Yet each may convey by his or her posture and facial expression what he thinks of himself, and his sense of self-confidence (though some are good at hiding it).

Just so with animals. Though they do not possess the gift of words, there are whole languages of signals, scents, and sounds that communicate both information and the state of their senders' emotions that we as human beings are just beginning to learn how to read. There are a great many ways of marking territorial borders, a few of which we have discussed. Sometimes an animal identifies his kill or simply leaves some sign that means "I was here." Birds

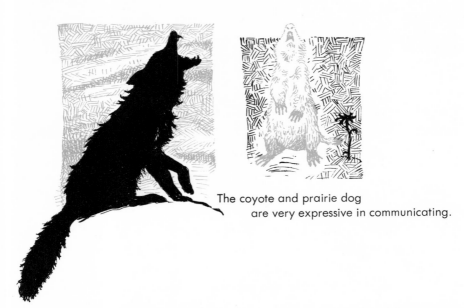

The coyote and prairie dog
are very expressive in communicating.

and mammals that are feeding often keep in contact with each other by small sounds, just as migrating geese keep up their rhythm of honking, especially when flying through clouds or fog, and elephants do by a low rumbling. Animals recognize members of their own group by colors, pattern, or (as ants do) by scent. Species have their own rich vocabulary, especially of scents, concerning the relationships between male and female, of courtship and mating, of parents and young. Even an octopus has a repertory of colors that surge across it, denoting fear and other feelings. Many crabs, fish, and lizards speak to each other by means of colors, gestures, and movements.

Touch is important, and personal contact can be a way of communicating. A lion lies with one huge paw slung across another lion, and zebras and wild horses nuzzle against other members of their herd. Monkeys and apes are commonly observed picking bits of dirt out of each other tirelessly, but some form of bodily care of one animal for another, called grooming, occurs in many mammals and birds.

Just as "one picture is worth a thousand words," it is said, a

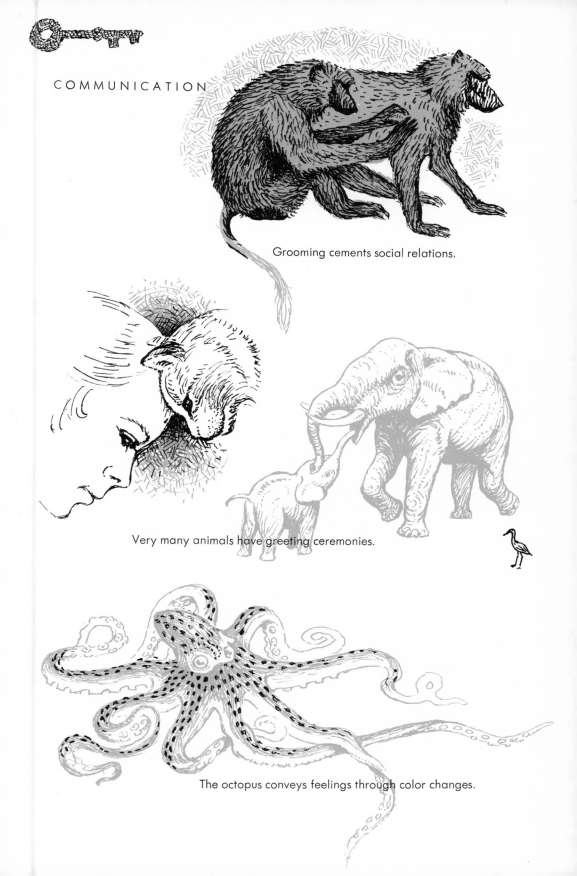

COMMUNICATION

Grooming cements social relations.

Very many animals have greeting ceremonies.

The octopus conveys feelings through color changes.

ceremony or ritual can take the place of an act itself. The way a wolf stands holding its head, ears, and tail, while looking directly at another, says "I am stronger, more self-confident than you!"— and a fight to prove it is avoided. The human fist held up or the hand held out for shaking are both silent messages that can avert a fight. A chimpanzee comforts another by patting its arm; an elephant gives many a caress with its sensitive trunk.

A social group is a unit that would crumble into fragments if the parts were not united through communication. Whether living alone or together, animals must make contact with each other or they would be as isolated as desert islands, with oceans between.

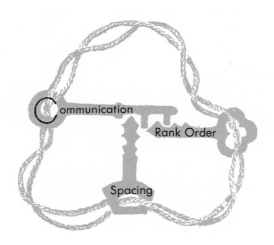

4. Bird Biographies

BIRDS FLIT and soar about; we catch glimpses of them as they flash in and out of our days. We hear a treeful twittering, like noisy fruits, as they prepare for autumn migration. But we see little of their whole lives sunrise to sunrise, and we know little of their companionships and sequences through the seasons.

There are birds that appear to live almost entirely alone—the owl seems the very symbol of solitude. But no bird can be completely solitary. The pair is the smallest social unit, though not all birds succeed in being involved in pairing. And there is a very basic fact of bird life: the young at birth are much more helpless than are offspring of other egg-bearers, such as reptiles, fishes, and insects. Some bird chicks can find food for themselves soon after hatching (ducklings, for example), but are still defenseless. Therefore all baby birds are dependent on much good care.

Two vital ties in the lives of nearly all birds enable the young to be raised in relative security. One tie is the bond of affection that holds mother and father birds together, sometimes for part or all the breeding season, but in a number of birds for life. Many bird parents, when the young are grown and flown, go each their own way, or are separated by their flights, the weather, or the hazards of food-seeking. Yet they find each other again when the time rolls around to start another family, as many American robins do. Our beautiful cardinals, "redbirds," usually remain together all year round as a mated couple.

The other tie is the strong attachment of the bird pair to a territory, be it a large space or just a few feet, or only pecking distance from the nest. In birds requiring larger areas, a food supply for the growing young is more or less ensured, as raiders of their own species tend to stay away. Thus the tiny wren may "own" a full acre of land, from which it chases away intruders. But the large king penguin in its crowded rookery occupies only a half yard or so on which one parent at a time takes its turn in the long, exhausting duties of warming and protecting the single egg or chick, while the other parent is off feeding at sea.

Most birds' social life takes different forms through the year. Nesting season is a very intense time. What a wide variety of family life it takes to get all the new generations raised to independence! At one extreme is the cuckoo and the cowbird mothers, who lay each egg in the nest of another bird, usually a smaller kind than she. The adoptive parents then need to hatch the egg left on their doorstep, so to speak, and to feed a very enormous little mouth. The birdling and new parents alike seem to feel they belong to each other. A far cry from this is the ostrich family. Here the cock collects something of a harem of hen ostriches. Each lays her eggs in the same collective nest, leaving the devoted father to do most of the brooding. He is given nest relief occasionally, but only by his Number One hen. It is also the papa who raises the babes.

There are more thoroughly single-parent families. The mother hummingbird builds her nest and cares for the young all by herself. Wild duck mothers likewise incubate their eggs and raise the brood alone, but in many mother-run families the father is somewhere in the vicinity guarding the territory against strangers and dangers. Yes, and there are other father-run families also. The liberated mothers, such as the female painted snipe, will have none of raising snipelets. The male of the large, flightless rhea, or "South American ostrich" (though not a true ostrich), not only chases away

Phalarope mother

father

the several females who laid from twenty to fifty eggs in his nest, but broods this large clutch alone for several weeks, and looks closely after his family for five or six weeks after they are hatched. Still another case is the phalarope, a small North Atlantic bird of sea or shore. In this unusual reversal it is the female, larger and more brightly colored than her mate, who leaves him to prepare the nest, incubate the eggs, and care for the young while she wings off elsewhere.

But the great majority of birds are "family people," at least during the breeding season. Two parents cooperate in the duties of brooding the eggs, keeping the nest clean, and feeding and teaching the young, though they may divide the duties in different ways. This is strictly an interaction between two birds who have chosen each other, and outsiders of their species are driven away. The male has selected the area first, chosen his nesting site, and in many cases announced his occupancy from prominent spots. The fiercely territorial mockingbird sings out his rapturous songs from atop television aerials and chimneys; the woodpecker's rat-a-tat advises other woodpeckers to keep their distance. Should an enquiring visitor advance closer, he can see the landholder's colors or pattern like warning flags. Should this chap (who may not have been able to find untaken land of his own) approach more boldly still, he can see the proprietor's intimidating display of feather-puffing or some other energetic action, which usually discourages him from further trying to take over. The female, arriving later from migration, is recognized by her plainer dress and/or behavior. She eventually settles down with him and a close bond grows between the two—

the pair bond that makes them desire to stay together while they share in the raising of their young.

Though they may drift apart later, some mates remain faithful to each other as long as they both live, as do most ducks, swans, geese, eagles, and perhaps many other birds of prey such as hawks; also penguins, many sea birds, house sparrows, chickadees, and some others are believed to.

A strange chapter in bird social relations reads just the opposite of their pairing off during breeding season. Instead, in certain species, males are attracted to each other's company to stage spectacular performances on dancing grounds. In this dance arena they may show off as individuals or as a group. Tall cranes on stiltlike legs make deep bows, hop and leap, turn and twist to each other or at times to the occasional female who leaves the sidelines to cavort with one or another of them.

How to describe the antics of birds in group courtship displays? Some may bound, vibrate, and stomp. The rosy flamingoes, their bodies crammed together sometimes by many thousands, prance and jig with snaking of long necks in a stunning sight, as they vocalize in a roar like continuous, distant thunder. Some performers pretend strife, rushing at each other at top speed to stop short suddenly, for serious fighting is not common. Some at the height of their ecstatic show suddenly freeze in a rigid pose as if someone had shouted "Statue!" The sage grouse and prairie chickens of

Sage grouse and prairie chicken in courtship display on "booming grounds"

western United States (like the Uganda kob) put on elegantly wild festivities on cold early spring days, with hundreds of males participating, each on his fought-for little tract of ground, each transformed into a gorgeous spectacle of feathered ruffs and adornments.

It is the interaction that counts. A kind of mass hysteria builds up. The presence of large numbers of their kind excites the males to greater frenzy, and stirs up the more lackadaisical females into taking interest in the proceedings. Alone, it is the mothers who then brood the clutch of eggs, care for the young.

If some 90 percent of birds use the loyal two-parent system of rearing the young, it must be a very successful way. Why, then, should some others employ different methods? We see that in the former, very many are tree or woods dwellers whose food seems to need more seeking after, with both parents required to find enough for the hungry mouths in the nest. In addition, the young are helpless and require much care, and eventual assistance in learning to fly from high perches. Parent teamwork is vital.

But in the single-parent system we find another set of factors. These birds are often dwellers in the open (brushy prairies, spacious fields). The parent that cares for the young, most often the mother, is a ground-nester. The baby birds are self-helpful (precocial) almost at once after hatching—it would go hard with them if they were not. It is among these birds that there are group-dancing males. Here in the open, food can be steadier in supply, easier to find in season. Again food and safety are weighed into the final balance. Thus:

—nonhelpless hatchlings can both feed themselves and
—be led by the hen into hiding from danger; also
—be kept away from crowds of cocks which might attract snakes, coyotes, and hawks.
—Fathers, therefore, are not needed for family care and so
—these performing lords, released from chores, have more time to compete with males and to court females.

There are also helper-birds among certain species of birds, non-breeders who may mate another year. These assist the parents in incubating eggs and feeding and protecting the hatchlings—unpaid nursemaids who labor tirelessly for their charges. Still another kind of cooperation occurs when the young of some birds graduate from nest to nursery school. Here a number of youngsters are supervised by one or several adults, as in the cases of such mammals as elk and wild mountain sheep. Flamingoes, for example, have bird-care centers where large flocks of half-grown juveniles band together. Older penguin chicks also gather in "creches" presided over by a few mature members. When father or mother return after weeks of feeding at sea, parent and chick find and pick each other out of the crowded, noisy multitudes—a truly remarkable feat of recognition.

Aggression—here we examine another very widespread, important interaction. We shall study it in one particular bird, the herring gull.

Very many sea birds live in large, even huge colonies. Exposed as they are beneath the wide, all-seeing sky, it is very practical that they find safety in numbers by living at close quarters. This discourages predators, and is also a vitally necessary way of sharing whatever little barren islands, rocky cliffs, or sandbars are available. Nor would it make sense for them to claim individual territories of an acre or a mile when they fish or scavenge over great areas,

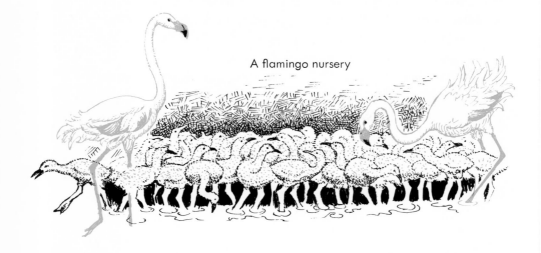

A flamingo nursery

Herring gulls

with vast seas and long shores for their cafeteria—feeding grounds which must be shared by all. Mammals and snakes sometimes steal their eggs; bird predators (raptors) attempt to assault them from the skies. The beautiful white terns post as many as ten or fifteen guards for a large colony, mostly against marauding gulls or piratical skuas, but warning or attacking all approachers. If necessary, the whole ternery will rise up in a screaming avalanche at a warning from the sentinels.

But crowded conditions impose other problems, and peace and harmony are not easily come by in such colonies. The much-studied herring gulls are strong birds, capable of good fights. How do they handle their social pressures?

In sea bird colonies what appears to be a confused mob is in reality an orderly bunch of pairs, each couple with its own small territory. Unmated young males group together here and there in "clubs." As gulls come and go on their daily rounds a returning pair sometimes lands on another's turf, and when the true residents return, trouble breaks out. Gulls have vocabularies of postures, sounds, and expressions understood by other gulls, who often collect around them like spectators at a boxing match. The threat posture of the property-holding male informs the squatters they had better take off without delay: great wings spread slightly, neck stretched tall, he paces stiff-legged toward the other male. The intruder, with upreaching neck thrust less forward, stands always at an angle to the owner, never facing him directly. Thus the males hold, threat posture against anxiety posture, until the intruder is usually first to sidle away in surrender. Or more of a skirmish may take place when the land proprietor charges at the challenger, who again usually takes off rather hurriedly.

Bluff fighting also occurs when two couples desire the same site. Either or both males tear up bunches of grass or moss, perhaps

47

waging tugs of war over the same tuft, as they take out their frustrations on the landscape. (Females less often participate in these encounters.) Sometimes two gladiators face each other with a peculiar tail-up tipping forward of bodies, jerking their heads rhythmically at the ground. This action can go on for some time until tempers cool. Sometimes a scene arises, with a side that is funny, but only to the human observer, says Dr. Niko Tinbergen, who studied these gulls extensively in The Netherlands. Two or even three couples sit near each other for a time, wearing odd facial expressions, doing their tipping-forward (as if pecking at the ground without touching it), and uttering choking sounds, while foot-scraping at the ground. Though minor clashes are common enough, and severe, all-out fighting with fierce pecking, hitting, and pulling by powerful beaks and wings does occur, these great birds can hold in check much antagonism through ceremonies that substitute for actual violence.

There are happier sides to relationships.

Pairing and nesting occupy around half of the bird's year—one side of a coin, very different from the other side, when relationships reverse as the breeding season draws to a close. In a bird's life, its fellows are rejected one time and sought after another. "Free as a bird" neither sex is when a parent, for both (in the majority of birds) are utterly bound by their two ties: to family and to territory, with all outsiders unwelcome. We saw that there must be a strong mechanism, an attraction of fondness, that binds parent birds together.

How does this arise? Let us say a male has arrived from migration, won his territory from rivals, and has vigorously driven off any encroaching species members. How is he to overcome his hostility toward others in order to attract, win, and hang onto a bride? The choosing of each other by male and female, the growing and gluing together of their interests, are stimulated by the age-old behavior called courtship.

48

The male courts the female in dramas often of intensity and strange beauty, all of deepest seriousness to the involved parties. (In a very few cases, such as that of the phalarope, a reversal of roles causes the female to court the male. Sometimes he is pursued by several of these ladies at once.) The house, or English, sparrow, common of city and town, displays his black shirtfront as he hops about, spread-winged, with energetic gestures like an excited tiny rooster. The peacock's dazzling performance before the pea hen is world famous. Drakes (male ducks) engage in group activities on the water, as these birds are still in winter flocks when they choose their lifelong partners long before mating season. The gorgeous mallard drake, for instance, fluffs out his bright feathers while dipping and raising his head and uttering strings of urgent whistle-grunt sounds. The red throat pouch of the frigate bird blossoms out into an enormous balloon, as its wearer soars over southern seas. Several birds exhibit dizzying stunts in midair in an ecstatic show, or plunge at breakneck speed to suddenly level off and glide again up to high altitude. And the blue-footed booby of tropical Pacific Coast regions, spreading his webbed toes, marches with proud steps before a female booby, who falls in love with his manners and his handsome feet.

The courtships of our more familiar songbirds, such as the American robin, are less spectacular and take closer watching. But we need not journey to Antarctica to watch the majestic bowing, posing, and flapping of penguins, or to Australia to marvel at the satin bowerbird arranging pretty pebbles, bottle caps, and blue flower petals on the ground before the bower he has built to attract a fiancée in order to study the spectacle of courting. The common pigeon, city cousin of the rock dove, struts before a seemingly indifferent female as the sun glints on an emerald-flecked and swollen neck of turquoise and royal purple. The whole course of their acquaintanceship from sidewalk to building-ledge nest is as engrossing as stalking a bird in the jungle wilds.

There is much left in bird behavior for you, perhaps, to discover

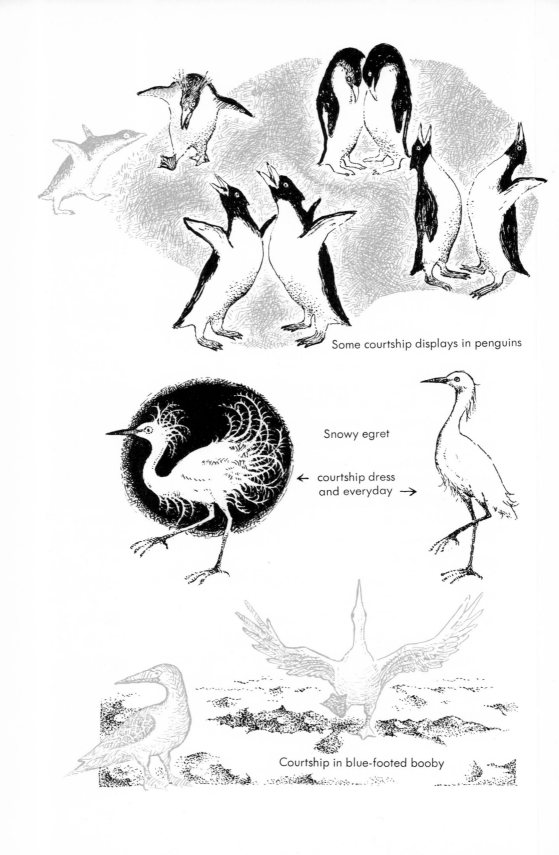

Some courtship displays in penguins

Snowy egret

← courtship dress
and everyday →

Courtship in blue-footed booby

the reason for. What is a convention of noisy blue jays up to, bouncing stiff-legged on branches, then suddenly taking off behind one member? Why does a galaxy of small shore birds take flight at the same instant, for no apparent reason, in a great loop out over the waves, to return to the same spot they left a minute or two before?

As the summer draws to a close (in temperate climates), the family birds that have excluded outsiders from their company during breeding season begin to turn into joiners for the other half of their year. Flocking is the real essence of birds together. Forgotten is the two-and-two of pairing, though many couples and even families, such as geese, do remain near each other. Now comes the call of a greater companionship, of a bond with the largest fellowship of all, in the grand event of migration. Millions of birds flood the skyways, southward in autumn, northward again in spring, flying along certain routes and much at night, when they are safer from raptors. Some travel alone or in small groups which often like to gather together when resting en route. Many thus form huge throngs that split up again when flight is resumed. Even more solitary birds, as some owls and hawks, become social.

Within migrating groups little organization or leadership seems necessary, and rank level seems also to be at a minimum. Now, in a calmer time, free of rivalries over territories and mates and pressures of raising the young, their behavior of aversion to others has faded, and even reaction to predation from hunting birds is diminished. All have a common interest. All are directed by a mysterious map of some sort in their heads, are pulled by some ancient call that says, "Follow, follow." Follow your own kind. Follow the guidance of the sun's direction even as it changes position crossing the sky or hides behind clouds; follow to some extent clues from the stars, and possibly other forces of the heavens or earth we do not know. Follow million-year-old routes to an entirely different life for a while, says the command in their heads, and then fly the compass needle back again.

Watch a flock some autumn or spring as it veers and wheels, testing its wings and nerves in taking off and landing, and wonder how, or by what or whom, are its individual members guided and united into something resembling one giant, miraculous creature with a single mind.

5. *A Word About Fighting*

WE ALL KNOW, or think we know, that many wild animals are usually eager for a fight, with their dagger-like teeth and ripping claws. Many stories and pictures inform us of their angry, bloody warfare. Even the rabbit has powerful kicking hind feet. "Fighting—it's the nature of the beast," we hear. Let us look into this nature.

No animal is likely to wish to suffer or throw away its life, though some do for the good of others. Over centuries past, the free use of their deadly weapons would have ended only in their wiping out great numbers of themselves, and the impulse of nature is to live, not die. Also, much of their emotion is turned into a ritual—making a sign or ceremony that takes the place of the real thing, as a man holds up his fist and thus averts a fight. His opponent thinks twice before attacking. An animal making a submissive, or surrendering, gesture before another may take a hunched posture with head turned away, tail down, and the superior animal will seldom use its advantage to attack. Thus much fighting is avoided. When aggressiveness takes place in the animal kingdom there are reasons for it.

There are two kinds of aggression: the kind between animals of different species, and that between animals of the same species. Little serious battling goes on between those of different species.

Two about evenly matched may vie for the same meal, but one or the other will flee the instant it feels it is about to be outdone. Predators tend not to like each other, and lions, hyenas, and African hunting dogs may fight with each other on occasion. But the two keys of spacing and communication, with warnings to stay off-limits, tend to keep others at distances. Heroism is not very practical if it costs you a bad injury or your life. Animals that flee or fight back, as the case demands, are exercising the first right of every creature on earth: self-preservation.

Most aggressiveness is between animals of the same species. Here as elsewhere there are inhibitions—inward sets of self-controls which hold back fighting except under certain conditions.

Females do not fight seriously very much, except for a mother in defense of her young. Then she will do battle desperately and fiercely. First she, too, will attempt to escape or hide with her offspring. Occasionally a wild fawn is seen in the woods whose mother does not defend it. Very likely she has gone off to feed and will return. Possibly it is so young she has not yet developed maternal or defensive instincts for it by licking and smelling it sufficiently.

Males versus females: there is little fighting here. A male baboon or chimpanzee may be rather hard on the opposite sex sometimes, but whether she likes it or not, she accepts it. With a number of spiders and insects it is quite a different story. The female, usually larger than the male, is programmed by instinct to devour insects. Her breeding partner, to her, is simply something eatable that moves, and he had better identify himself and his intentions satisfactorily before mating, and make a quick get-away afterward.

Male to male is where the most serious conflict is found. It can happen over space. Many mammals, lizards, and some fishes will defend their territory or homesite to the death if need be, though such disputes usually do not end that way, as bluffs and threats are sufficient. Birds especially, as we discovered, will defend their share of the landscape and avoid fighting both musically and honor-

ably. Howler monkeys shout and roar in treetop choruses for the same reason—daily ceremonies addressed to other troops of howlers which keep them from encountering each other, and thus stave off monkey-war, which could be deadly at their green altitudes. In most kinds of animals, however, where there is unnatural crowding, there is a great deal of fighting. Normal inhibitions vanish, males attack females and each other, both sometimes attack or abandon the young, and there is much abnormal behavior.

Hard fighting also centers around females in nature. Though such combat may occur over a particular one, such as a grizzly bear defending his spouse from kidnappers, it is more often a contest to see which male will stand his ground most formidably, which will send the other running first as soon as one recognizes a superior. Excessive energies in the rut, or mating season, of hoofed animals are outrageously fierce, and a deer buck will thrash a small tree to splinters if he cannot find something that will fight back. Wild bighorn sheep stage stupendous battles where horns clashing upon horns echo for miles among mountains and cliffs.

Fighting is not to kill. Certainly there are very bad injuries and

55

there are deaths. But the aim of each combatant is to force the surrender or flight of the other. In fact, predators use their fearsome weapons in different ways when fighting for social reasons than when killing game for food. It is true that we do not understand the motives of some fights that end fatally, as between two lion or rhino males, but these are not common. It is hardly likely that animals comprehend death; they wish only to subdue. Rarer still are the animals who set out to tear up or conquer another group or destroy the helpless. This intention is probably unknown to beasts. Man alone finds glory in warfare and takes pride and pleasure in deliberate causing of pain and death.

6. *A Word About Killing*

Yes, animals kill each other. We may not think pleasantly of the tiger that leaps upon a graceful antelope, of the hawk that snatches up a helpless rabbit in its talons, or a snake gulping down a fluffy duckling. Such innocent deaths might be considered cruel and vicious.

Pictures of wolves in particular have reflected the hatred of predators by man: the wolf seen as a bloodthirsty beast, eyes aflame with hate, tongue dripping, fangs gleaming, as it demolishes a gentle and soft-eyed deer. A tender little girl in a cape and red hood about to join not-so-tender granny inside the stomach of a single 125-pound animal. But the wolf, the hawk, the snake do not kill in hatred. They are hungry.

Pangs of an empty stomach operate on both the inborn and practiced behavior of an animal, causing it to attack its quarry expertly. Even so, many more attempts at catching a victim fail than succeed. This gnawing hunger is a far more urgent matter than the appetite of a person (who probably breakfasted only a few hours earlier) ordering a hamburger for lunch, which he, likewise, does not attack in hatred or rage. Furthermore the predator, be it tiger, hawk, or wolf, is probably incapable of understanding the pain of another creature—only human beings can do that. All deal the death blow, in whatever manner, as quickly as they are equipped to do so, since animals cannot afford to waste their energies in delay, but seek to conserve them. The African wild dog, for long shot down by man as a despised, ugly killer, does not make destroying its victim a lovely sight. But we need to understand that this is a smallish animal that can survive only through the cooperative methods of pack-hunting. All animals kill the only way they know how. The lion, considered more attractive, hardly has more considerate methods. Predators are unable to turn themselves into fruit and salad eaters. Man the Predator is more able to do so, but not likely.

There are other gross misunderstandings. Pumas and coyotes (also wolves and grizzly bears, before they were exterminated from most of our states) seen dining on cattle and deer have often been eating a carcass they found dead or dying of disease, injury, or old age, though they were accused of its demise. Predators seldom kill wantonly but only when they need food. Hyenas stroll in leisurely fashion not far from wildebeests, who sense that they are not now hungered after. Most predators usually consume their meal thoroughly. Others bury what they do not eat, returning to it from time to time. Still others eat in relays; the jackals take over from the lion and hyena, the vultures have their turn, on down through the last traces by the beetles and bacteria. Though in some cases animals overkill—because an excess of food is available or, in other instances, we do not know what motivated them—this in no way compares to the thousands of men who have left heaps of giraffes slaughtered, untouched but for their tails taken as trophies, or mountains of elephants killed only for their tusks; of American bison slaughtered by millions nearly to extermination for "buffalo rugs"; of uncountable animals pursued by helicopter or snowmobile until they dropped in their tracks, for "sport." One man wrote of rowing his boat down a tropical river in South America and shooting a splendid jaguar swimming for shore up ahead, because it made a good target.

The weasel seems harder to defend, as it does steal barnyard fowl and kills ferociously, leaving much of its victim untasted.

But on investigating further, we find this to be an intensely active little animal with a prodigious need to refuel its body often, since it burns up energy at a great rate. This gives it a craving to satisfy its keen hunger rapidly. Being small, it does not require a great amount of food at a time, but is off soon, and by the time its hunger flares up again it is elsewhere, and forgotten is where it left its lunch. It does sometimes bury its overkill for future use.

Even the large meat-eaters subsist on small animals and insects, as well as carrion at times. Wolves, foxes, and coyotes can keep down populations of mice, rats, ground squirrels, and woodchucks that would run all out of bounds across the countryside without them. When prairie dogs and other such obtainable food are killed off, as with poisons, or their land is taken for other purposes, predators turn to livestock. In addition, all animals, if not killed, must eventually die of natural causes, and the flesh-eaters clean the land of their bodies that would otherwise litter the earth. The services they render pay their debt of the occasional sheep or calf stolen in hunger. The hawk, though it may sometimes kill a quail, consumes large numbers of rabbits and rodents that would take a great toll of farm crops otherwise.

The prey needs the predator as much as the other way around. Numerous studies have shown how carnivores, when they attack animals as large as moose and elk, single out the weaker, the less able, who would spend a longer time dying of exposure to bad weather and of starvation. The predator is unlikely to look for trouble by trying to combat a strong animal who can fight back. Human hunters aim for the handsome and healthy, disdaining the sick and old. Watching a pack pursue its quarry is to marvel at the way an animal at a disadvantage, including the young who cannot keep up, are separated out unsparingly. Though we view this with anything but enjoyment, we must admit that, in the long run, it is the strong, those in the prime of life, who remain to pass on their best qualities to their offspring, and thus the herd and the species are made fleeter, stronger, and keener.

Against the predatory animal man has a huge case of vengeance

People have always loved a scarey monster story.

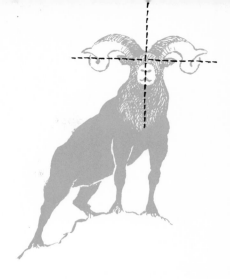

which he seeks to justify; to "punish" these culprits by near-extermination. Call it some strange rage or pleasure of his own. Mistakenly he feels that the hawk or wolf takes animals he himself wishes to hunt. The wolf itself is not a threat to man, but seeks to hide or flee as rapidly as possible, as do wild cats and bears. Our vendetta probably began when early human hunters, in dim ages before recorded history, huddled around glowing embers together. In the darkness of long nights they shuddered and shivered over horror tales of giant carnivores charging down upon them, defeated in the nick of time by the heroism and superiority of man. Such a story always ensured a spellbound audience.

Call the predators varmints, or brutes, or villains. Call them wicked killers. But get to know them first.

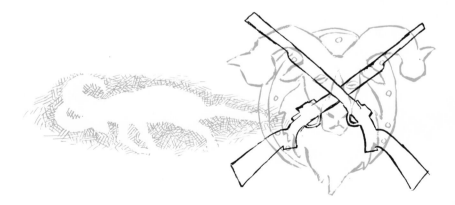

hunters

hunteds

SOME
LAND
MAMMAL
GROUPINGS

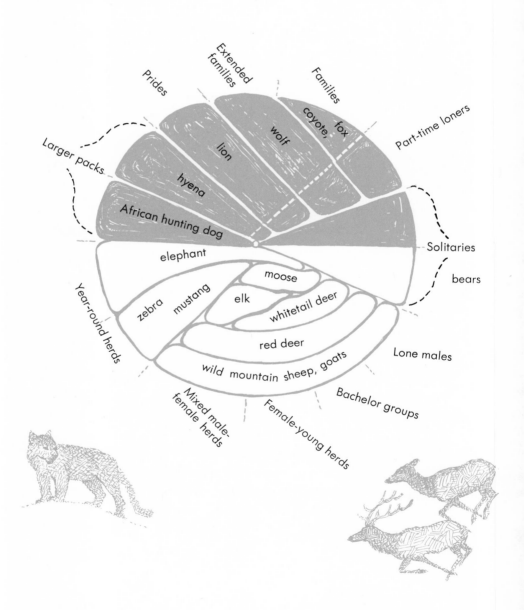

Prides

Extended families

Families

fox

coyote,

Part-time loners

Larger packs

lion

wolf

hyena

Solitaries

African hunting dog

bears

elephant

moose

Year-round herds

zebra

mustang

elk

whitetail deer

red deer

Lone males

wild mountain sheep, goats

Mixed male-female herds

Female-young herds

Bachelor groups

7. *Hunters and Hunteds*

THERE ARE hunters among animals, and there are the hunted ones. Needless to say, their lives are as different as day and night; each is half of the whole. Their every tooth and toe, to say nothing of their senses and digestive systems, fit their ways of life. Their bodies have been studied for many years, their behavior for a much shorter time.

THE HUNTERS

Hunting animals have not been very easy to observe, both because of their naturally private ways and their having learned fear of man. Captives have been studied in zoos wise enough to provide them with somewhat natural habitats, and by people who have had occasion to raise some from a very young age. Other studies have been carried out in the wild. The ethologists who have done so have rarely found it necessary to carry firearms. Of the fascinating quantity that has been learned, we tell only a little here.

Let's join a wolf pack. Here are some adults stretched out in the sun, over there a heap of cubs tussles and tumbles. A full-grown wolf approaches another with more positive bearing, and is met by a raised tail and fixed stare, which cause the first to avert his gaze,

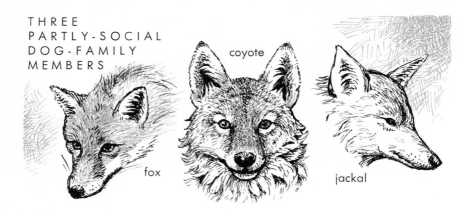

THREE
PARTLY-SOCIAL
DOG-FAMILY
MEMBERS

coyote

fox

jackal

turn his head away, and stand hunched with tail lowered. Still another male keeps a watchful eye on the youngsters at play, and he does not happen to be their father.

This group is not simply a bunch of animals hanging around together. This is an organized society, and if we could observe it long and carefully enough we would see what a complex group it is, each member with a role to play.

It is late afternoon. A few run out of the campsite a way, their exceedingly sharp noses testing the air. Back they come, and all adults throng around the Number One male and female to engage in a mutual outpouring of licking, tail-wagging, affectionate pushing and shoving with expressions described by observers as closely resembling smiles. From this demonstration they will derive information and solidify their bonds of closeness and cooperation that will unite them in the hunt to come.

Now they begin their march, single file—most of the adults, not quite all. Here is a she-wolf remaining behind, near the den where the cubs have retired to huddle up in sleep. She does not happen to be their mother. The large, handsome male has taken the lead and the silent line heads off into the dusk, measuring their trot for distance. They may cover as much as forty miles tonight.

Dawn is beginning to color the horizon. Tired and full, the returning band lopes back into camp. The cubs, lively and hungry, romp up to two adults they recognize as their parents and sniff, rub, and nip against their muzzles. Both adults regurgitate a quantity of meat onto the ground which the cubs devour. This is the grown-ups' way of carrying food back. And now the adults have stretched out for some well-earned rest. The cubs are five weeks old, and today's play will be some of their school lessons to them.

Raising the cubs is a pack affair, for how else would the younger members learn how to interact with the group? Cooperation is vital to their survival. From three to thirteen weeks of age is their crucial schooling time. By chasing and mock fighting and tugs of war they learn who is most strong, and how to use and control their strength against stronger and weaker. They learn where each fits into the rank order. When seven months old they will be ready for lessons of a new sort, for they will be of age to begin going on hunting trips. They must be able to keep up. The campsite will be abandoned.

Any adults may bring back food to the mother while she is denned up with her newborn bundles of fur. When later she comes out to hunt with the others, both parents plus aunts and uncles deliver meat to the cubs and whomever stays behind with them. All pack members must learn to know each other by smell and appearance. Touch, too, has been important to their relationships, from the curling up together of the small pups to the later contact of rough-and-tumble. They learned obedience early so that they might learn techniques of tracking and hunting with the others later. They learned to read many signs of weather, geography, danger, and of other creatures.

Animals living in groups have a wide range of expressions of faces and bodies. Even how and where the hair stands on end at times reveals emotions. The lone-living bear is not nearly as expressive as the wolf. Carnivores have more facial expressions than most herbivores (though the fruit-and-leaf-eating monkeys and apes are exceptions), as certain muscles in their faces are more developed. The important fact is that wolves form strong bonds of affection to their group-mates, learning this in their crucial first three months.

A crew of brawling, quarreling members would not survive long.

We can see resemblances in the dog, related to wolves, in its look of devotion to its master, its loyalty sometimes to extremes, the droop of depression and loneliness it is capable of. Wolf puppies can be trained by experts who know wolves, but these animals belong in the wilds, neither chained, caged, nor confined in any way, for wild living and freedom are forever in their blood. In wolf behavior some facts fit together rather in a circle of logic. We see that:

—these large carnivores that hunt as a pack
—need large prey to feed them; therefore
—they must cooperate together, which also
—diminishes fighting among themselves, which leaves
—more of them to survive as a group and hunt as a pack.

Now to Africa, where we shall observe another formidable hunting group, which we would expect to be the lions. But no, it is the hyenas. These have long been scorned as cringing cowards, scrounging their meals by stealing lion-killed leftovers, or scavenging on the carrion of forest and plain. But the hyena is no beggarly, walking garbage can. Hyenas can be efficient hunters. They form deadly packs, doing a turnabout with the lions, for instead of being snatchers from their table, it has been found that even

Hyena mother and cub

Hyena male female

oftener, in some places, it is the lion who takes what by rights belongs to the hyena.

There is another surprise here, a reversal over wolf pack structure. For it is the she-hyena who is stronger, larger, and heavier than the male, a state of affairs extraordinary among vertebrates, the animals with backbones. Furthermore, there is a strong dominance hierarchy or rank order here, and it is the highest-ranking female who holds sway over her clan and leads it forth on expeditions and hunts. This also is very uncommon among carnivores. There may be as many as forty members in a hyena clan, possibly up to one hundred. Because they are sometimes solitary, sometimes social, hyenas need all the more to recognize each other and renew old ties with effective communication whenever they meet. Hyena clans have definite territories, though boundaries shift and change, and battles are occasionally fought over them. Border patrols, led usually by a female, trot around the boundaries daily, rubbing a pasty, smelly mass from glands beneath their tails on tall, stiff grasses. Hyenas also use large areas over a period of time for defecating, or depositing their droppings. These are whitish when dried and very visible, strongly advertising the clan odor—a hard-to-miss warning to trespassers. A hyena party out on a hunt leaves droppings along the way, possibly also to warn others to stay clear of this zone.

Fathers and all mature males generally keep away from the very young, and mothers, though attentive to their own cubs, do not share in raising those of others. As the cubs grow older there is

African wild dog family

much visiting around from den to den and much staying overnight, for all the world like school chums. Cubs at an early age learn polite gestures to adults: lifting their hind leg for a quick sniff by each elder, and giving a sniff or face-lick in return.

African wild dogs (Cape hunting dogs) have very close-knit ties of affection, with all males taking a much larger part in cub raising than do hyena fathers. A great event is the emergence of new pups from their birth den for their first appearance in the outside world. This occurs around the time they are a wobbly three weeks of age. What a frenzy of excitement boils over as all pack members, including older cubs, seem to go crazy in a dizzying celebration, nosing each cub over to lick its undersides, racing from one to another who is still trying to regain its unsteady feet, while all make their peculiar twittery sounds. For their first few months the cubs seem the property of the whole pack, almost more than of the mother. This denning time is the only period when these nomads of the plains stay fairly settled for a while before moving on again across their huge range, which may be 1,500 square miles or more.

All members bring food back to the den mother and regurgitate it, or to whomever replaces her as nursemaid to the cubs. When the only female of one pack (usually there are more) was killed, all males continued to carry food back to the nine pups until they were old enough to begin traveling along. Little fighting goes on among wild hunting dogs. At a kill they are practically polite to each other, and adults make sure the pups get fed first. There is male leadership here.

Like the American wolf and spotted hyena, African wild dogs have complex relationships among them. All three have greeting ceremonies, most often after separations and before setting out on hunting expeditions. These vigorous and excited rituals increase the sense of awareness and belonging to each other, and of cooperation which puts pack welfare above the interests of the individual.

The King of Beasts also presents some surprises. The lion is head of his group, or pride, it is true (a position often shared with another or several males). But it is also true that, although lions often hunt alone, it is the queen of the pride who leads on a hunt, older cubs usually following next, while the kings bring up the rear. The lion system is different from the wolf system.

Consider how cats are made. Dog-family members are runners and chasers. Wolves often take turns at the front of the hunting line in relays while the leaders fall back to restore their strength and endurance. But cat-family members tire more quickly. They are made for the silent, slow stalking, the tireless, patient wait, the sudden lightning-leap or powerful pounce when the prey is either captured or makes its escape. Young house cats at play reveal these traits.

Most lions live in prides of a few to thirty or so members, averaging ten to fifteen. The pride is seldom found all together at the same time, as some members scatter through the home area. Nevertheless it is a closed group, usually intolerant of others who try to join up. Adult lionesses remain with the pride throughout their lives, but after a few years the restless males often rove elsewhere.

Members sprawled at rest present a homey sight with much grooming and rubbing against each others' golden bodies, the mitten-pawed cubs playing and scrambling over the patient grown-ups, snapping at their switching tails. Now late afternoon's shadows grow long and it is time to think about getting dinner. There is much yawning, stretching, and ambling to feet. The cubs do not join in active hunting until going on a year of age. In communal hunting there is a certain amount of maneuvering, of spreading out in utter silence with the result that the quarry may be driven rearward to the catchers in the backfield.

Cubs often have a hard time growing up in lion land. The mother keeps her blind and helpless newborn well hidden among rocks or heavy foliage for their first few weeks, returning to them between hunting trips. But Mother likes the pride, to which she may return too early and neglect her cubs; likes hunting, necessary to everyone's survival; likes devouring what she can before her lord and master dives in for his share, when much argument goes on over the flesh. The cubs, when they tag along, must fight for their rights, snarling to get and hang onto whatever bits they can snatch. It is not their mother who usually provides for them at these times; surprisingly, it is a male who may seize a portion from her and allow the youngsters to have some.

But what shall we think of the lordly creature who lets his womenfolk do nearly all the work of hunting, while he is first to take fresh meat they have obtained—he who even may rob hyenas of their kill? He seems more like the Cowardly Lion than the King of Beasts. But judging animals by human standards is not reasonable.

Seen in his maned splendor from afar, he is a recognizable silhouette to others as he maintains possession over his territory, and is a source of protection for his pride. But seen in this magnificent mane (which protects him from slashes and biting), trying to sneak up on swift and alert prey through grass and brush, he is too easily spotted by zebras and wildebeests, "a moving haystack," as one ethologist described him. The sleek female is made for slinking unseen; he is not.

And what of a mother who may desert her helpless cubs, who later allows them to eat only what they can snatch at a feast? The social system of lions seems less developed than do those of wolves and wild hunting dogs. But it is the mature female who must stay strongest and best fed, as it is she upon whom the pride depends for food, and on the male for land-holding and security. There can be more cubs. The laws of nature may be harsh, but they are time-tested for survival.

The Hunteds

Balanced against the flesh-eaters are the hunted animals. Alone or together, they had better not be caught off their guard. Yet zebras graze calmly enough where lions saunter not far off, and a wolf trots across a steep mountain meadow a few leaps away from a wild bighorn sheep.

The carnivore, as we know, gets its nourishment from consuming the plant-eater, whose body turns grass, leaves, fruit, and bark into flesh. The meat-eater must chase and subdue much of its food, which may hide from it or run fleetly or fight back. The food of

Lion order of march

the herbivore stands and waits for it, so to speak. While consuming it, the herbivore itself may be sought after. And so the bodies and behavior, minds and emotions of hunter and hunted must be very different.

When a small, tasty meal for a hunting animal—say, a rabbit—wishes to feed, it usually comes out by evening, hiding during the day, eating and living more or less alone. But what of the larger, daytime herbivores which graze in the open? These are mostly the hoofed mammals, prime food for the predator. Both need each other, as we have seen.

Cities, highways, and increased building have taken most of the countryside that was once the habitat of wild animals and have altered their ways. But here we look as much as possible into their natural mode of living—the ways they were conditioned to live before man affected their ways so greatly.

Growing up and family living are very different stories for the young herbivore and the carnivore cub. A ranger in Alaska (quite a loner himself, it seems) once brought a wild bighorn sheep he rescued, only a few hours old, to his remote cabin where it soon became a pet that leaped about on chairs and bed. When only two and a half weeks old it was able to follow him thirty miles over rough ground and in icy weather. Two-week-old caribou of America's Far North have been seen keeping up with their mothers while chased by wolves, and little wildebeests of Africa must be able to keep up almost at once after they are born. Contrast these to young wolf cubs whose eyes have barely opened by two weeks, and lion cubs of this age just able to crawl.

What different family scenes we find among hoofed animals! While fox and wild hunting dog fathers and uncles expend much care and labor to keep all cubs supplied with food, the horned and antler-bearing fathers probably do not even recognize their own offspring. Stupendous rams, bulls, and stags are here, sporting magnificent headgear. But do we find them to be the royal monarchs of the herd? And for that matter, what is a herd?

72

A herd of wild bighorn sheep of the Rocky Mountains is for most of the year a society of females with their lambs. There is some organization and cooperation. While most ewes are off feeding on some other slope, a "baby sitter" stays behind and keeps an eye out for the lambs at play. From time to time a lamb baas out a cry; the mama replies from afar, and the nursemaid also sends a call across the wide spaces: "All is well." The rams are off in other high pastures. Sometimes a fortunate human being will spot an awe-inspiring line of fine bachelors poised against the sky on some far crag.

At even higher altitudes, wild mountain goats live, climbing among jagged rocks, and tightrope-walking along knife-thin ledges in hair-breadth places. Up here the nannies, too, care for the kids in separate small herds, apart from the more free-living billies most of the year.

The American elk (more correctly called wapiti) are social animals, forming herds which are sometimes quite large. The leader, an elk cow, is usually the oldest one in the herd. Heading her company of other cows with their calves of different ages, she finds the way to forage along trails which she alone is best able to remember. First to make the decision of where to cross a stream or road, and experienced in the surest ways to escape danger, she

Wild mountain goats

is sharp and keen to all signs around her. Often elk calves, too, are left with a nursemaid elk. An observer once counted seventy in one nursery!

Moose are less social. They are so enormous that adults do not need the protection of being in herds. There are mother-calf groups in which the cows defend their young ferociously from danger. Most males simply wander wherever they please within their range, free to be alone. Yet these bulls are often found in each other's vicinity. Perhaps this is just where the good grazing is; perhaps they like each other's company—who can tell?

Skipping over the ocean we find high adventure in the Scottish Highlands. Far up on misty mountain meadows, in the shadow of peaks with such names as Sgurr Fheon and Beinn Dearg Mohr, where the wild winds play tricks with clouds and whip up waterspouts from the crystal brooks below, live the red deer (similar to the American elk). It was in the 1930s that Sir Frank Fraser Darling set up tent, lashing it down tightly, in the weather-swept haunts of these very social deer to make one of the first, excellent studies of animals in the wild.

Sir Fraser, even learning to stalk the red deer barefoot in the two years he spent in their rugged domain, found the many scattered herds to be made up of female-run families. There were the milk hinds, or mother deer, with their newest calves and their yearlings, and the near-adult young maiden hinds, as he called them. Females always remain with the herd. The staggies, or young adult males, may stay on a while or leave to go out on their own, where they form bachelor groups. Full-grown stags themselves are in loose sorts of companies that change membership, with no par-

An elk nursery

ticular leadership or structure about them.

But the hinds are well organized, and they have a leader. "Herself of the Long Neck," she was known to woodsmen, for it was she who thrust forth her head to sense danger, ever alert. She is the oldest female, the sharpest-witted and most intelligent one, with much wisdom remembered. The welfare of the followers can override even her need to eat. There are Number Two and Number Three hinds after her, and on down the line in ranking order. A watchful rear-guard hind is on duty even, when the herd travels or is in flight.

Now comes the season of the rut, for it is autumn. This is the few weeks when males are most male, feeling their strength come into them to beget offspring. They had shed their old antlers last April and have grown new, larger ones. There is fighting among them, mostly great-muscled shoving and lunging, and though there are injuries (few of them serious), the stags put on more show and noise than real violence. Their necks have grown thick and powerful; they have acquired voices for the only time they will have them in each adult year.

A stag may travel some distance to reach the herd of his choice. Perhaps it is the one where he was born. Arriving there and flushed with gigantic energy, he puts on a glorious performance of running and charging. He cuts the younger bachelors and lesser stags out of the way, and rounds up groups of hinds by twos and threes until he has amassed a harem, possibly a very large one of sixty or so and their followers. Now for a time they belong to him, and to him alone; let no other try to steal the harem-master's property! Around and around the group he races and roars, then whirls, and charges back the other way, stopping but a few minutes now and then to catch his breath.

About a week has gone by. He has expended great energy and has mated much. He has eaten little more than a few munches of moss. He has grown exhausted. And so our stag leaves his harem and climbs up to high hilltops, toward the mountain peaks, among blowing clouds and raw winds of late fall in the Highlands. Here he cools down for a few days of near-solitude, up where stags are peaceful toward each other should they meet. And then, rested and restored, he descends at a fast clip over rough ground, perhaps to cover ten or twenty miles—back to his harem, which he may have to try to win back from some other stalwart harem-lord. For the winner, it is a case of "the fastest with the mostest."

But Herself of the Long Neck is never off guard. Let danger threaten—perhaps men with guns or, in times past, wolves (now gone), or a heavy, early snowstorm which she often somehow senses in advance—and she gives warning. She barks; all pay attention. Raging harem-masters, now meek as lambs, with the hinds and calves, follow under the charge of Herself, led by her deer-wisdom over rock terrain, across hurtling streams, through pine woods to greater safety. The herd is a matriarchy, and we see again a female reigning among hoofed animals.

American elk bulls join the herd in late September, keeping harems of seven or eight females. The cows, usually peaceful, become tense and nervous while bunched together. These bulls do not put on quite as spectacular a show as do red deer stags. Bison (buffalo) bulls also have been living apart from the cows until the time of the rut. Now they, too, collect a harem which they tend, keeping other bulls away with prodigious shows of head-tossing, circling each other, and head-slamming. Heavy fighting itself would send them into the hard western winter weakened and ill-prepared, and their disputes do not often come to really lethal fighting. For all their masculine bravado, we find elk and bison herds also usually led by the experienced old female. Moose, though massively antlered, do not round up harems but spend a few days with one female and then on for a partnership with another.

And across the vast, barren tundras of Russia, great herds of reindeer have been seen to be led by the most worldly-wise and experienced she-reindeer.

76

Reindeer

What of our beautiful whitetail (Virginia) deer? They are quite another case. We catch a glimpse of a doe and her fawn slipping into the woods at dawn, or two or three whitetails in an abandoned apple orchard at dusk. But where are the herds?

Some old-timers (human) have recalled that long ago they saw deer in herds or in long lines, single-file marches, led by a self-assured old doe. It is possible that white man's ways drove deer back into the forest's dark protectiveness where there was more seclusion from bullets and farm dogs. Consider forest living. This is a way of life where group-dwelling offers little protection—in fact, may call attention to the hideouts of social animals. Consider their communication. Among trees and heavy foliage group members are unable to tell friend from foe always in time. They cannot keep contact well by sight unless close together, cannot flee so well if their group is discovered, cannot send and receive messages of cocked ears and tall heads amid underbrush and tree trunks—though a flashing white tail may soundlessly say, "Follow me!" Sounds of warning travel best among trees and through darkness, but concealment, near-solitude, and silence go best with safety.

There is a peculiar stomach arrangement found in many hoofed animals which is of great value to them. They can swallow their forage with no chewing of it and bring up this "cud" later, to masticate it thoroughly. Re-swallowed, it goes through four stomach compartments and onward for the rest of its digestion. The secretive whitetail can thus emerge from hiding at evening to browse in woods openings and meadows where better food

Whitetail deer

grows, catching its food on the run, so to speak, and retreat in safety to chew its cud later at leisure.

But in winter when snow may make travel hazardous or impossible, deer tend to gather in "yards." Now they need each other. Here many hoofs trample snow into paths; many eyes, ears, and noses are alert for signs of danger.

Safety and food are again weighed against each other: more safety, less food. Trees become badly overbrowsed; all reachable twigs and bark are devoured. Deer often have a very hard time of it in winter. Now is the season for predators, also very hungry. The weak, the old, the starving deer, those that would be a longer time dying would now fall prey to wolves, even coyotes and to wild cats as nature was once balanced.

Let us journey over to Africa once again. Will the great herds of zebras that roam the grassy plains resemble in any way those of elk and red deer? We find no suggestion of the wise old female, or matriarch, who when necessary leads an entire herd. Instead we find herds made up of scattered families—but families with a difference. These are close groups that stay together throughout the year, where the father reigns supreme and the young adults leave only after several years of growing to maturity. The stallion is a loyal harem-master, usually trotting alongside or at the rear of his family marching in line, which is then led by his Number One wife. The other five or six mares follow always in the same order

stallion

Zebra order of march

lead mare

behind her, their one-, two-, and three-year-olds in that order behind each. But in case of being pursued or attacked by a posse of lions, hyenas, or wild dogs, as the mares and young flee toward safety, the stallion whirls to face the aggressors with bravery and ferocity, rearing up and lashing out with fast-flying hooves.

As does the wild horse stallion back in America. Once again to our Far West, where the noble mustangs gallop (as long as we can keep them alive and free). These one-stallion bands also contain a harem of several mares with their foals and yearling colts. Here a lead-mare has second place behind her harem-master and here, too, he protects his band, remaining to face and valiantly combat any threat that appears. This band-master is stern and strong as he herds his harem with signals, such as stretching forward his head, while weaving his lowered neck back and forth with no-nonsense meaning: "Stay close! Get in line!"

Food and safety—safety versus food. Most hoofed animals are out in the open much or all of the time. Head down to feed, a wild bighorn or wild horse yearling could be surprised and attacked alone. Together with others, alertness can be shared by many. Wolves coming upon bighorn sheep have been met by rams bunched together, stupendous horns at the ready. Zebra stallions

Zebras grooming

Pattern: herd or harem

Principle: too many unneeded males together may consume too much food.

Pattern: pack living

Principle: all hands needed
for cooperative hunting.

Pattern: usually solo living

Principle: food size and quantity
sufficient only for one.

Pattern: two parents

Principle: it takes much teaching
       and learning for way of life.

Pattern: one parent

Principle: father not needed
        for care of young.

Pattern: bachelor groups
        or lone males

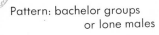

Principle: males can take
        more time to attain
        maturity and strength.

wild and free

Mustangs

also will sometimes mass in a semicircle to face marauders: a striped but solid wall of defense.

Here is the pattern: one male to several or many females. One stallion to his mares all the year, one stag or ram to his harem for a briefer season. But where are all the other stags and stallions, bucks, bulls, and billies? There must be a number of leftover males that do not reproduce each year, if some have more than their share of females. This is true. Each year many males do not reproduce because they are younger, or less strong and impressive, and cannot stand up to the greatest of the males. Females usually reproduce as soon as mature; males generally have to wait one or many years to win a partner. Here is where the once-a-year voice of some, the handsome size and power, the showy crowns come in (though the function of horns and antlers is not certain; occasional males without them seem to do quite well). There is angry, ferocious action of bucks as they lash out at small trees, clash at each other's heads, and thrash around on the ground, in wallows of dust or mud from which they get up looking and smelling marvelously. Some tear up vines and tangled grass which trail from their antlers on the autumn winds, proud banners proclaiming their fearsome state. Mustang stallions rear up on hind legs to hoof out and bite at each other. Thus they interact together, to impress and interest the females, but mostly to intimidate and show off their malehood to their rivals. Each strives to vanquish competitors and captivate the most brides.

It does not sound fair. There should be enough of everyone to go around, to make proper families. But again: animal behavior must not be compared with human beliefs of morality, as we see how the system works.

—Herbivore females need much time for carrying the unborn within them and raising the young, and

—fathers are not needed to bring food to them, so

—one male can spend a little time mating with several females. Therefore, it can be seen that

—fewer males must be stronger, in order to get, keep, and sometimes protect mothers and young, and therefore

—it is the best of the breed which pass on their strengths, speed, and wits to the new generation.

8. *The Great and Powerful*

THERE ARE animals with such enormous weight to throw about that it would seem that nothing would dare try to prey upon them —animals that require such immense amounts of food it would appear that only solitary ways of living could possibly serve their needs.

We find that the largest living creatures of sea and land are not only mostly social, but likewise that these greatest ones are generally gentle and peaceful beasts. Whales are mammals which nurse their young, and are descended some 40 or 50 million years ago from land-living ancestors. Most live in small family groups or larger pods, these often spread out over their vast watery spaces as parts of greater groups, the way chapters are parts of a whole book. The pods, the families, even the solitaries coalesce in the great migrations northward and southward, many congregating in massive aggregations, often after fasts of many months, at their feeding grounds.

There are hunters and hunteds in the seas also. Though porpoises and dolphins (both small whales) and their larger relatives pursue schools of fish, the killer whales, known as "sea wolves," are feared predators of seals, dolphins, and of whales much larger than the killers themselves. They form cooperative packs, knifing swiftly just below the surface, rising and falling in unison as they bear

84

down on their prey and close in on it with merciless efficiency.

Though a few whales tend to be solitary much of the time, and the largest creature on earth, the blue whale, forms family groups of parents with single calf, most live in herdlike structures. These are cow-and-calf groups with a few "aunties" about who are interested in all young calves and are helpful to others. There is usually a bull not far off, who, as with sperm whales, swims around the group, keeping an eye on it, while submature males roam farther and wider in their own clubs.

Needless to say, whales and their relationships and behavior are difficult to study. Could our ears hear underwater as theirs do, we would hear their complex communication, for possessing poor senses of vision and smell, they move through worlds of sound. Their messages carry over great distances. A rhythmic droning can read, "I am a gray whale, separated from my group, desirous of rejoining you wherever you are." Another call: "Blue whale calf! Stay close to me, your mother!" Or from afar off, "Sperm whale injured and in much distress, urgently needing help." Humpback whales and dolphins are especially communicative choristers, and are also playful and boisterous lots. Complicated devices are required for underwater study and recording of these voices.

As in a game of Blind Man's Buff, touch is almost as important as sound. Whales are very tactile, and their sense of feel, stroking each other with flippers and gliding close alongside one another,

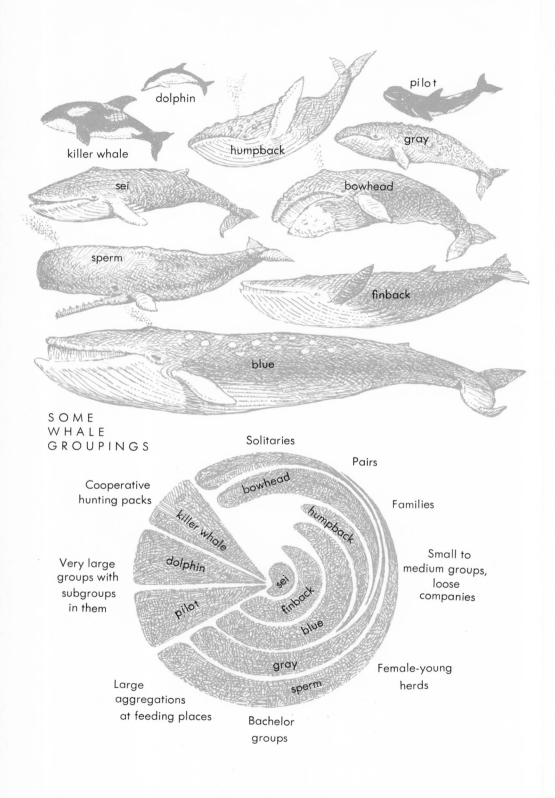

dolphin

pilot

killer whale

humpback

gray

sei

bowhead

sperm

finback

blue

S O M E
W H A L E
G R O U P I N G S

Solitaries

Pairs

Cooperative
hunting packs

bowhead

humpback

Families

killer whale

Very large
groups with
subgroups
in them

dolphin

sei

Small to
medium groups,
loose
companies

pilot

finback

blue

gray

sperm

Large
aggregations
at feeding places

Bachelor
groups

Female-young
herds

goes with their affectionate natures and their pleasures in contact. There is much sensory life and sensitivity in the tough hides of these great, benevolent beasts.

Elephants, interestingly, follow a similar pattern we have seen before, though one with a truly extraordinarily high social development. The basic unit is the cow-calf herd, with "aunties" in plenty. These are immature or adult females that are childless for the time, who help to look after the young, like the mother, with fondling and fussing. This close family is led by a powerful protective matriarch who will throw herself into the face of danger at the front of her herd whenever necessary. Submature males remain with the herd until some twelve or more years of age, when they gradually fare forth to join bachelor groups. Here they struggle for dominance in the rank order with mighty shoving, wrestling, and intimidation. The great bulls themselves often roam alone. Though with less strong ties than are found among their cow and calf kin, bulls have relationships among themselves also, as when they perform greeting ceremonies after absences from one another.

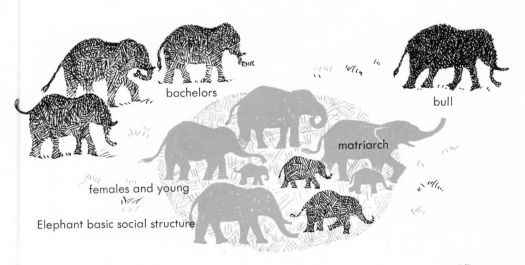

bachelors

bull

matriarch

females and young

Elephant basic social structure

Altruism is the helping of another.

Ponderous as they are, healthy adult whales and elephants have little to fear from animal predators (though a very great deal from man). Slowed down by calves, they do need to defend themselves with clever strategies, as killer whales can attack and destroy ambushed adult whales of much greater size than their own. Whales will often remain at the side of a badly injured companion, even attempting to raise and hold him or her at the surface to breathe, though this act of devotion may cost them their own lives.

Tigers, lions, and others enjoy eating small-elephant, and older elephants wall in calves for protection among them, in one of their many cooperative acts. Elephants rally to defend each other with ground-shaking stamping, smashing of bushes, throwing up of dust, trumpeting, and threat attacks. As many as sixty-seven, mostly females, have been counted in a magnificent defense of one member. Coordinated demonstrations attempt to raise a dying fellow, while the powerful matriarch hurls herself back and forth between these heroic efforts and suspected danger.

Both whale and elephant young have long growing-up periods (at least nine years for a sperm whale, twelve or more for an elephant), and with quantities to learn. What wonder, then, that the adults, who may live sixty or seventy years, develop strong individual personalities, learn to recognize and remember all kin-folk in their range, and grow strong ties of affection with each other?

The others of the huge and powerful all have their life stories, in many ways the same, yet different. Group-living repels most rhinoceroses. But rhino calves, for all the suits of armor they seem to live in, do not discourage lions from considering them choice eating. Mothers defend their young with the ferocity of wartime tanks. But for what reason, we may ask, does the white rhino mother keep her baby usually ahead of her, while the black rhino youngster follows its mother close at her heels?

Hippopotamuses, largest land animals on earth next to elephants, believe in nothing if not togetherness, bumping and nudging each other in the African waters where they spend most of their day, with apparent affection. They have dominance relationships among them. As for the greatest and tallest, giraffes exhibit less social structure than hippos in the loose group-living they practice. In general, adults seem to drift together, attracted mostly by good browsing and good company. It is the younger set, the juveniles and teenagers, who form clubs of closest bonds.

9. Our Nearest Relatives

A CHIMPANZEE, wearing a sailor suit, cavorts around a circus ring on a little tricycle. A gorilla beats his chest and roars fiercely before flinging a strong man through the air and capturing a maiden. A monkey swings swiftly across tree limbs—or cage bars. In these ways we get a false picture of the private, natural lives of monkeys and apes, which together are called the primates. This group includes mankind also, but here of course we consider only the nonhuman ones. Though they, especially the apes, are our closest relatives in the animal world, their normal ways of living are not the ways of cities, circuses, and zoos, and few people know of their behavior in the wild. What of the real primates of forest and grassland, their days, their nights, their secrets of living— alone or together?

Most primates are shy, peaceful, and agreeable creatures, preferring to live their lives well hidden and distanced from human beings. Only a few kinds have gotten used to dwelling near the habitations of people. Even the gorilla, famed in legend as a horrendous monster, is still another victim of highly untrue publicity. Primates are far more likely to remain hidden or to disappear silently at the slightest hint of man in their vicinity than to allow their presences to be known.

They are nonetheless very social creatures among themselves, most living in groups of one or another type. For all their intelligence, advanced beyond that of probably all other animals, their societies are not necessarily more complex in structure than are those of certain other mammals. There are different kinds of groupings.

Not many primates are loners. There are a number of small, primitive ones who hunt for fruit and insects by night, alone, though they like to curl up to sleep with others of their kind (bushbabies, pottos, mouse lemurs). Orangutans, large apes of the tall trees of Borneo and Sumatra, are the most solitary and unknown of all primates. They are not well understood, are difficult to study, and are faced with very possible extinction in the not-far-off future. There are suggestions that they, like many another animal, may once have lived in larger groups but under much persecution by man have learned to retire to what secret strongholds they could hang onto, as silent, evasive shadows.

Next there are two-parent families—a father, mother, and one or several young of different ages. The gibbon, smallest of the apes, floating on its long arms through treetops of Southeast Asia, lives in small, loyal kin-groups, closed to outsiders.

Larger troops of all sizes are the commonest style of primate living. These are not the noisily wrangling gangs they appear to be when crammed into zoo cages, but are organized societies. Many contain harems. Extra males are in bachelor groups, or just circulating by themselves, usually around the edge of the group.

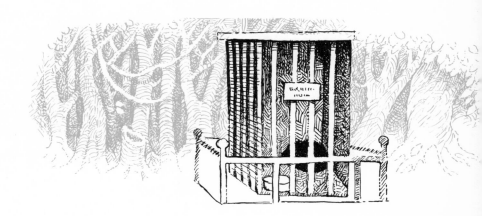

Howler monkey

Howler monkeys of central and South America, the temple monkeys (langurs) of India, and baboons of Africa live in such troops.

Gorillas, largest of the apes, also do. One or a few older males and two or three mature but younger ones, several females and their offspring, form a sort of extended family. This moving community, not often changing membership except for births and deaths, travels about feeding on plentiful vines, bark, and leaves. The youngsters chase and tumble with each other while the adults doze in the sun—altogether, when not harrassed by man, a pleasant life. The dominant old leader makes decisions about moving on, resting, and nesting (mostly on the ground), and he keeps peace and harmony among them. Should the pathways of two troops pass near each other, the groups may feed close together or may even mingle their numbers for a while before separating out to continue on again, each in its own direction.

Females of whatever kind of primate seldom wander or mix with other troops. We see that most primates live in societies of stable relationships.

Except the chimpanzees. No harems here, for adult males mate with any adult female who will have them, and females are free with their favors when they are in estrus. Mother-offspring groups tend to band together, however, and males and childless females form a second type of party. But there is a flexible openness about chimpanzee groupings, which split up and exchange members and re-form as these remarkable apes shift from one set of companions to another. If you are a howler, gibbon, or gorilla,

92

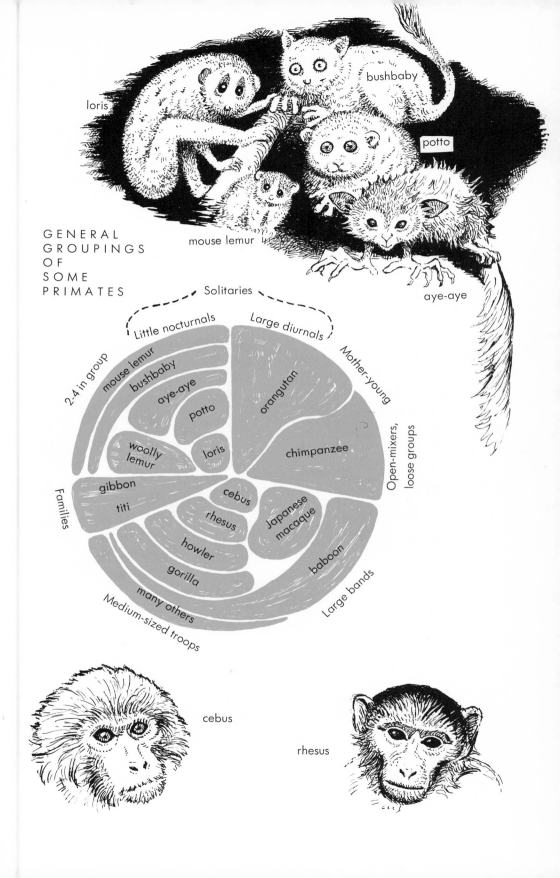

loris

bushbaby

potto

mouse lemur

aye-aye

GENERAL
GROUPINGS
OF
SOME
PRIMATES

Solitaries

Little nocturnals

Large diurnals

Mother-young

2-4 in group

mouse lemur

bushbaby

aye-aye

potto

orangutan

woolly lemur

loris

chimpanzee

Open-mixers, loose groups

gibbon

cebus

Families

titi

rhesus

Japanese macaque

howler

gorilla

baboon

Large bands

many others

Medium-sized troops

cebus

rhesus

you are a belonger mostly to your own exclusive club; if you are a chimpanzee, you recognize all other chimps in the vicinity as fellow travelers through your part of the jungle, and somehow feel a larger loyalty.

Basic social structures, then, are very different among primates, with the solitaries, the parent-pair families, the stable troops, and the open-mixers. There are certainly reasons behind the "choice" of lifestyle of each species; each group follows the way of living that has worked out best for its survival needs, though there are many aspects of this we do not understand at present. We can consider how food-getting habits and safety need interlock—but could there be more explanation?

We might expect to find small, insect-eating primates needing to chase around alone for their nourishment, as each food-find is just one partial meal for one stomach, and therefore they have to hunt at night, for safety's sake. We do find this in the huge-eyed, see-in-the-dark little bushbabies, pottos, and lemurs. We can expect daytime feeding and social living to go together, when animals can see each other, can feed in company, and need to hide less. So we discover that tree-dwelling, diurnal food-seekers who eat fruits when and where they ripen do dwell in small troops—gibbons, and the titi monkeys of South America. Fruit here and there in season on one or a few trees at a time does not serve too many customers. We could expect to find a diet growing on both trees and the ground to supply larger groups—the chimpanzees—and larger bodies—the gorillas. We could expect to find animals that eat a varied diet of fruit, leaves, grass, insects, and even occasionally meat, which are found spread out across the plains, able to forage in largest gatherings—baboons.

We could expect to find animals living in year-round groups cooperating, as wolves, African wild dogs, even killer whales, and some other animals do. We do not find this so often in primates. They read the signs of others discovering and eating, and follow their example, but it is every ape or monkey for himself, and they do not commonly offer food to their companions.

There are many hungry mouths to feed on monkey meat—leopards, lions, pythons, boa constrictors, some meat-catching birds. Not many primates do become food for predators, however. Even so, again it is a matter of having to balance food against safety.

Consider some opposite aspects of group-living that must be weighed against each other. Advantage: more food is found by a whole tribe scouring the countryside, peering into ravines, poking behind bushes and boulders, than by one animal alone. Disadvantage: there are thus more individuals to use up available food faster. Advantage: a larger troop contains more eyes and ears to guard against danger or a bigger protective army to stand between foe and fleeing females with young. Disadvantage: a larger congregation of animals is more conspicuous to hungry hunters from afar off than are a few. But it may also be that a larger number confuses, say, a cheetah who cannot decide which one to chase and dashes this way and that.

Let us contrast the private lives of two kinds of baboons. The desert baboon (the great-maned hamadryas, or sacred baboon of the ancient Egyptians) lives on arid reaches of northern Africa where food, especially in dry seasons, is sparse. At night large troops huddle together on cliff faces, hopefully out of reach of prowling leopards. There are no big trees to sleep in.

A large troop is made of smaller bands which may travel several miles a day to their eating places; the bands, in turn, are made of harem-families each under a male. Woe betide the careless female who strays very far away from his watchful eye for very long. He is a strict master (though more relaxed in later life), and his group, with their young, breaks away from the other one-male units to forage for food by themselves when the whole convoy reaches its destination. Thus they spread over a wide territory to avail themselves of whatever food there is to be found, each one-male unit close unto itself, separated from the others. Even when with the entire band or troop, rarely does a unit-male look at females other than his own, though his own ladies may engage in flirtations with unattached bachelors. The unit leader had better not catch them at it or they are chased back home fiercely with sometimes a swift bite on the neck delivered. From childhood each female is taught to follow and obey the young male who sooner or later practically kidnaps her, taking good, actually motherly, care of her long before either of them is interested in mating. Thus the subadult males collect a few females for their harems over a period of time.

It is interesting to compare these and the savanna baboons. No closed, one-male units exist here; rather the males and females interact quite freely. All females lavish their affections on all infants —or attempt to, though the mothers of the newborn jealously try to prevent others from touching, fondling, or examining their new arrival for a while. (Desert baboon females look longingly at infants in other units but do not often succeed in getting very close to them under the watchful eye of their male protector.)

Why do we find such striking contrasts in closely related animals? The larger savanna baboons, foraging together in a mass, need to hunt food less assiduously than their smaller relatives, and are more mindful of safety out where grass and scrubby bushes sometimes conceal predators. The smaller desert baboon, needing food the more, takes greater chances against predators. No male

Desert baboon

tyrant who oppresses females needlessly is this stern leader, for it is he who may have to defend his family alone from a leopard, and so all are rigidly trained to remain near him and to obey, so there will be no wandering casualties when the units fan out to forage.

Primate infants are not only very helpless when born, but remain dependent for longer than do most other animal offspring. They receive excellent care, for the mothers carry them carefully and groom them often. Many adults and older juveniles play with them as they grow older. Young primates learn how to swing on vines, how to judge safe branches, and how to take death-defying leaps (not all do this) high above ground. They must study how to become good mothers, followers, group leaders. There is much of group customs and traditional behavior to be learned, and where each young animal fits in.

Adult males are more variable in their attentiveness to the little ones. Some carry infants about, some groom them, others play with them. Still other males mostly ignore the youngsters, though they protect them when necessary and even rescue them in the face of accident or danger.

The baboon male is physically mature around four years of age, the gorilla at ten or so. But primate males, though able to reproduce and almost fully grown, are not socially mature until some time later, usually having to go through a several-year period of waiting and preparing before taking a responsible place in their social group.

Savanna baboon order of march

True, food-getting and safety needs help hold monkeys together socially. But for two apes, chimpanzees and gorillas, there is usually little food scarcity and rarely are they preyed upon. Yet they stay together in regulated societies. There seem to be less obvious ingredients in their reasons for together-living.

Only among monkeys and apes, of practically all backboned animals below human level, do we find members that can breed so many times a year. The mature female primate's body is ready not just once or a few times, but at intervals of every four or five weeks, though she does not breed as long as she has a youngster that requires much care. When males recognize a ready female by such signs as an enlarged or reddened rump patch or other ways, they too will then mate, not having to wait for the twelve-monthly madness of the rut, or the late-winter urges of the fox or beaver. With infants born at any time of year, with females,

Orangutan

Gibbon family

males, and young of all ages interacting together, interests, group concerns, and friendships apart from mating and child-care can develop. The fawn, cub, or birdling that must be able to fend for itself in a few months' time cannot know the luxury of a long growing-up period, groomed, nurtured, fussed over, during a span of several years. More can be learned; knowledge and experience can be passed on, and the group grows in richness.

The wolf male may never take another mate if his own dies or is killed, and the hippo, fox, elephant, and some others may remain at the side of a dying or dead comrade. Beyond practical needs of food, safety, and child-care in many animals, there are bonds of affection, bonds of companionship.

Primates like each other. As do wolves, and wild horses, but the more arduous and limited lives of these four-legged mammals do not allow them the advantages enjoyed by primates. Observers note

how monkeys and apes derive pleasure from contact, from grooming and touching, from simply looking at each other with their
close-set eyes, seeming just to wonder about each other. Perhaps
in their dark tropical forests and wide, open savannas, with less
pressure for survival upon them, arose the possibility for more
leisurely intermingling combined with the seeds of thoughtfulness
that foreshadowed human intelligence and social concern.

10. The Unsociables

THOUGH THERE are many advantages to living in organized communities, still a great many animals dare, or care, to live alone in ways that work out best for them to do so. Animals in social groups have to show respect to at least some others. They often have to yield their place to higher-ups or await their turn at eating, drinking, and mating, and to travel when others do. But in exchange they receive advantages, as we have seen. They benefit by help and protection in a multitude of ways. There are many accounts of dolphins and larger whales who have received distress calls from sick or injured members of their species and have gone to their aid, even trying to hold one at the surface to breathe. Zebras will slow down their pace for an old or crippled member, and ten were once counted leaving the herd to thunder back to the rescue of a mare with her yearling and foal desperately ambushed by hyenas. Elephants try to lift or prop up a wounded or ill comrade, and whole herds come to the aid of a besieged fellow.

But "lonely as a cloud" the bear roams. At least he is alone; we cannot tell if he is lonely. He or she needs no bear-group to give it safety in numbers. But he does need food, as we saw. Any food. A grizzly will dislodge enormous stones or tear up a whole room-sized plot of turf with huge enthusiasm in hopes of capturing one small ground squirrel. If he can procure an elk or bighorn sheep, so much the better, but such a meal, when adult, healthy, and alert, can escape him easily enough. Bears steer clear not only of their own kind, but of human beings. But people can mean camping and cabins, and food lying around, and although people can mean danger, the food often calls out to them more loudly than the danger does. Should a number of bears come upon a good food-find around a picnic table, their way is not to share, but to ignore each other as much as possible and then to snap and snarl. It takes much food for each big body. Hostility needs to be a part of their behavior, as closeness would deplete the food supply each needs.

Solitary and secretive are most of the wild cats. Only the lions live in true prides. In North America the elegant mountain lion (puma, cougar) is too shy and remote for its habits to be well understood. From northern mountain fastnesses to desert's distances the puma stays as far from man's dominion as possible, attacking livestock only if near starvation. Like the coyote, it helps keep down populations of smaller animals, and it culls out weakened and old deer and elk.

Though large cats such as the puma, leopard, cheetah, the jaguar of South America, and tiger of Asia do not usually fight to defend their vast landholdings when strangers of their species enter upon it, they space themselves out so that meetings do not happen often. All place communication signs for eyes and noses to read. A puma scrapes leaves, twigs, pine needles, even snow onto a pile which it then urinates upon. Other pumas, seeing and smelling this, have been observed to sniff and study it, then backtrack along their own steps to avoid the maker of the scrape. Tigers often also defecate on their scrapes, which are deposited in conspicuous locations, such as along roads or passes through the hills. Many of these cats have two special glands beneath their tail with which they can spray scent backwards on trees and bushes. Though cheetahs and others scent-mark in this way also, it is more to leave information that "I was here," and others can take their chances crossing territories which are too large to be patrolled or guarded closely anyway.

THREE
CAT
SOLITARIES

Canada lynx

Bobcat

Serval of Africa

Though these mainly solitary animals are difficult to find and observe (in spite of tales to the contrary that they never miss a chance to leap upon passersby), they are not always so nonsocial with each other. Some congregate in gatherings which seem not to be organized; these cats simply like each other's company, at least now and then. The shy cheetah, that sleek, doglike streak of lightning on Africa's plains, can be seen lounging in the sun with other adults. Though no one is quite certain why cheetahs do not form organized hunting bands (nor why they are so scarce), it is speculated that if they were organized they would be so deadly and efficient they would wipe out too much game for their own good. Reports tell of jaguars resting in groups, where fairly safe from man, in remote back-country jungle or pampa.

Tigers, also, live and hunt mostly as singles, as far as is known. But they, too, are not entirely unsocial, and not only tolerate others roaming fairly near them often enough, but are suspected to like sitting around together occasionally. There are good reasons for their lone-living. Much of the game they catch is fairly small, and there are no herds for bands of tigers to prey on communally, as in Africa. Cats may like each other's company but it is often to their advantage to maintain wide spacing, and through their language of scents, sounds, and sights they respect the not-far-off presence of another as if by some Bill of Rights.

Beyond the bears, the wild cats, the orangutan, there are the

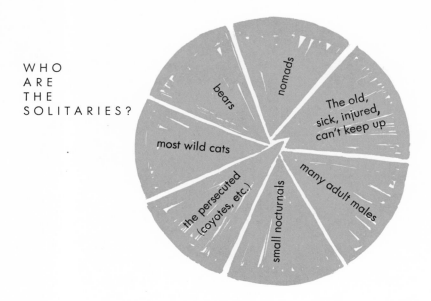

nomads

bears

The old, sick, injured, can't keep up

most wild cats

many adult males

the persecuted (coyotes, etc.)

small nocturnals

gypsy-wanderers from many social species that choose to take off from their groups, living more or less by themselves. Often they are old and probably tired, perhaps just no longer feeling like trying to keep up. There are the too-many who have been injured by guns and traps. "Rogue elephants," notorious for smashing down whole tribal villages, have been found to have a severe toothache or other pain, or to be going through a two-week period of excessive irritableness, a sort of madness they cannot help, associated with the yearly draining of the *musth* gland on each temple in males. The few tigers that "turn man-eater" may have had their usual reticent behavior altered by a gunshot wound. A fair number of lions become homeless globetrotters, some of them forming close companionships. Many of these no doubt could not find a territorial area to settle on, but others simply seem to prefer a gypsy's life.

There are whole worlds of small mammals. Rarely seen by day, they are mostly nocturnal, or night-feeding. They are in the low, dark places of the woods, the holes in trees and homes in hollow

104

logs, of burrows underground and tunnels through tall grass and beneath the snow. Though they generally seek food alone, some curl up and sleep with others through cold winter weather, as do raccoons and skunks, for example, sharing a nest in a corner under an old bridge or shed, or retreating into a woodchuck's burrow. Opossums and others are often by themselves except for mother-young groups caught sight of slipping into the brush or weeds, but we know little else of their spacing, their recognitions, and interactions with each other.

But alone or together, animals do not find all their lives serious. There is play! At times, when they feel safe and full, they can be seized with a carefree exuberance, some dizzy silliness that brings even the most solitary ones together for moments of something

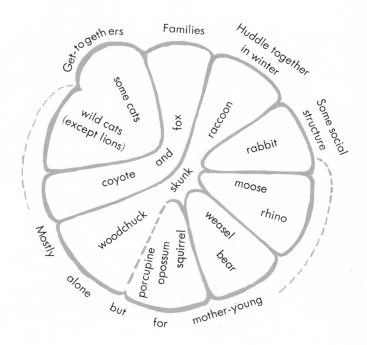

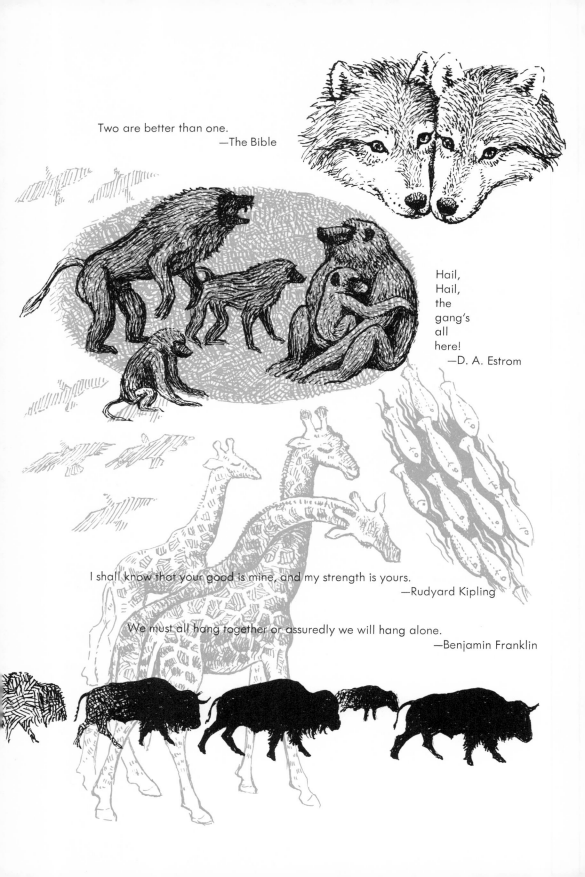

Two are better than one.
—The Bible

Hail,
Hail,
the
gang's
all
here!
—D. A. Estrom

I shall know that your good is mine, and my strength is yours.
—Rudyard Kipling

We must all hang together or assuredly we will hang alone.
—Benjamin Franklin

He
who
travels
fastest
travels
alone.
    —Rudyard Kipling

Solitude . . . is to genius the stern friend.
          —Ralph Waldo Emerson

I am never less alone than when alone.
          —Scipio Africanus, c. 150 B.C.

The strongest man in the world is he who stands most alone.
          —Henrik Ibsen

like leap-frog and tag and follow-the-leader. To their games there are no goals, no prizes. No one wins nor loses. Many hoofed animals simply take off and gallop around and around, and goats run up a half-toppled tree trunk to hurl themselves off the end, each in turn. Lions wrestle and grapple with each other, with no blood shed. Wolf cubs and elephant calves tumble and play-fight. These are times when animals can butt or whack at another and act totally foolish, as chimpanzees do, without penalty. Play—a great letting-go, important to every life.

Birds sometimes soar and glide in the golden sunlight, going nowhere, and fish have been watched from boats as they capriciously flashed about in water-dance designs, glinting and gleaming. Birds and fish have no other apparent motive at these times than of reveling in a burst of well-being that bathes them in the pure pleasure of the air or water that uplifts them, body and spirit. Dolphins and larger whales, surprisingly graceful, frequently engage in mighty marine spectacles of delirious arching, plunging, and splashing.

And of the quiet-living small solitaries, there are also those who frolic and caper, though it is not easy for mortals to catch them at it. Often it happens at that hour just before or at the dawn when little cottontails race and chase each other about on the dewy grass, and even fat woodchucks have been seen to frisk and tumble. Now hostilities and fears are vanished for a while, and loners have come together for fun. Foxes cavort and bound high in some moonlit forest clearing, and badgers at nightfall somersault and shove each other in games of king-of-the-hill.

Play. Even porcupines do it. A brief, precious time when animals are set free from the demands of living, and who can say they do not experience true joy?

And so we have seen when it makes sense for animals to trade the advantages of the group for private ways. There is no protection in an open crowd for smaller animals: hiding is safest. There is usually no advantage in uniting to find food, or of raising the young folks.

There are more than these understandable reasons for solitary or social living to be found if we delve more deeply. Scientists have been uncovering the complexity of ways by which populations of animals are kept steady in nature over periods of time, the way things were balanced by nature. We know that one species or another is not likely to multiply unchecked for long and "take over," as there are controls which keep total numbers within bounds, without mankind's manipulations.

From the nonconformists—the lone wolf, the dropout gorilla, the maverick lion—there may be good consequences. These individuals may profit, at risk, by finding new food resources in time of scarcity or a fresh water hole in time of drought. Herds and packs can be slowed or tied down by small members, or made captive by their allegiance to a land range or territory that otherwise offers them security. Perhaps a loner will be among the few survivors if disaster, such as flood or avalanche, strikes the groups. Yet the single baboon or elk may be seized by a wild cat, or a nomad lion may never find a mate who will have him. All take their chances. Perhaps by wandering far and wide some single animal will mate with a distant one in a breeding that, in combining diverse qualities of both, a new and stronger species will get its start.

Perhaps some nonsocial animals are simply different, and seek to satisfy something within themselves by wandering their wilderness in solitude. Perhaps they would have been troublesome and disruptive to the group had they remained. Both social and solitary individuals give and gain some advantages, and lose others. Each contributes in its own way to the river of life, whether alone or together.

Play

11. Some Practically Perfect Societies

CERTAIN GROUPS there are which come closest to functioning in ideal harmony and cooperation. We might expect to find such bliss among the highest vertebrates, the birds and mammals, but it is not there. This close-knit degree of efficient social organization is discovered in rather surprising places.

A jellyfish is perhaps the last place we would expect to find a system where individuals coordinate their activities more smoothly than masterfully made clockworks. Among the Siphonophores, a fairly common division of these dreamlike sea creatures, one bobbing, pulsating animal is in reality many jellyfish individuals, called zooids, living as a single unit. The largest member of this colony is the balloon-like, gas-filled float, its top and most visible part. Some species may possess several zooids, or "swimming bells" which work as motors, causing the jellyfish to dart, loop, or feebly swim by their contractions. (The float zooid causes it to rise and sink.) Other zooids are the tentacles, long or short. These dangle beneath the float, many containing the little stingers which can be painful to human beings. The most famous Siphonophore, the large, so-called Portuguese man-of-war, may have tentacles as immensely long as sixty feet, which bear stinging capsules dangerous to bathers. These paralyze and entangle fish and other catches and raise them to stomach-like zooids which do nothing but digest food. Male and female parts are separate zooid subpersons on the same jellyfish.

Hard-to-believe communities! No zooid can live alone, but only as part of the whole, as it has the power to do only one task. All are therefore interdependent. Each has subordinated its individuality to the good of the whole. The little half-dollar-sized Velella, its small sail fluttering, can often be found tossing in Atlantic shallows. Though all members of these strange colonial forms cruise more naturally in deep waters, many find their way toward shores.

It would seem an odd jump from the Siphonophore jellyfishes to completely unrelated insect societies, strange almost beyond belief in their own ways. Most insects live solitarily, as do the majority of beetles, butterflies, and grasshoppers. But when we look at the ants, bees, wasps, and the termites, we discover the only true social organization to be found among insects, where something like miniature cities operate with incredible efficiency. We will take a quick overview of them.

Female parents of lone-living insects scatter their eggs or lay them where they will hatch near a food supply, and that is usually the last the mother knows of them. But with group-living ones, there is a big, essential difference that we can compare, interestingly, with the habits of the highest vertebrate forms of life. For the social insects, with intense dedication, tend their eggs and the help-

Velella

less, white grubs that hatch from them. First, these are in their mother's care when a new colony is begun, and then her offspring stay on to take over attending to their younger siblings until there are hundreds or even many thousands of them. In contrast to birds and mammals, it is not a case of one parent or two rearing their own offspring, even with the help of a few "aunties" or other group members. Insect societies are more like a large and truly communistic state, where all the many young are the shared concern of the whole group in one way or another.

Now we encounter a second crucial fact of these insects' existence: job specialization. The nursemaids, for example, are specialists in their tasks (though they may graduate to other positions later). They even feed their tiny charges on the special food each kind requires, be it seeds, wood, honey, meat, or other nourishment.

It would have taken a vivid imagination to have invented the great diversity of ant workers which exist. Ants live in just about all land areas of the globe except polar regions, with some of their remarkable Lilliputian civilizations nearly everywhere for human giants to wonder at and observe. In addition to nursemaids, there are workers who engage in handling of food and dead prey, and who manage the cleaning-out of the nest. Some labor at digging out more ground chambers, others are outside construction experts around roof and tunnel openings. Still others forage for food. There are warriors for defense of towns, and soldiers that wage wars of offense. Some species have honeypot ants which store honey inside them until they look like golden grapes.

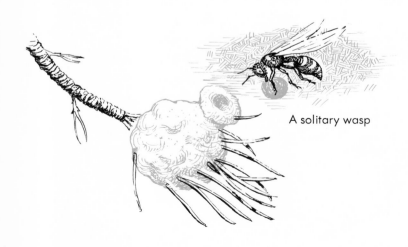

A solitary wasp

A few ant species are primitive tribes which attack and devour fellow ants savagely, often fighting among themselves with little group spirit. But most cooperate to an extreme degree. There are ants which hunt game—other insects—and two or more of these predatory pack members cooperate in carrying home a victim too large for one to deal with. Army and driver ants strike terror into four-legged mammals and even human beings in their path when they are on the march, so ruthless are they in destroying animals which to them are large as mountains. There are marauding troops which capture other ants for slaves, forcing them to do their drudgery for them.

More advanced than the hunters are colonies of ant dairymen which herd smaller insects, mostly aphids. These are readily found on some plants in summer. The aphid cows are "milked" for their sweet honeydew and receive protection in return. Also advanced are seed gatherers that reap and store their harvest, husking the seeds and disposing of the chaff. There are farmers that grow underground crops. Perhaps most remarkable are tailors that sew leaves together with fine, silken webs to construct waterproof nests in trees.

Now we find that of these hunters, soldiers, and tailors, all are females. Even the herdsmen are herdswomen! Each ant clan is, in fact, a huge sisterhood, all united under a queen. She does not actually rule in the sense of leadership; she is the mother of them all. The workers are sterile; none will ever produce eggs herself. Eventually a crop of reproductive females, and also males, are produced by the queen. Some of these will mate, the females to fly forth and try to begin new colonies, the males, alas, to perish.

Let us make a peculiar comparison: that of a very socialized ant commune with a far-off Siphonophore jellyfish. Both are colonies made up of laborer-specialists. But they fulfill their role to an extreme degree. The human teacher, doctor, or store clerk are all alike in basic anatomy. Nor are there working castes with different structures among any other mammals or birds. But each Siphonophore zooid-person shows no resemblance to those of different professions next to it. Among ants also, their form fits their function, though they resemble tribe-mates more than zooids resemble theirs. Ant size and body build can vary quite a bit; head and mouthparts are hands, tools, or weapons to them. Individuals of either kind have lost their capacity to survive separated from their group, whether actually attached to it or not. Even ant queens become so specialized they lose the power to feed themselves.

Though bees and wasps have fewer kinds of specialists, they, too, have both simple and complex social groups. (There are also solitary bee and wasp species; not so with ants and termites.) The young are raised in hives or nests which are architectural marvels. Here also are only daughter-workers, almost none of whom reproduces. These, too, are united under their queen-mother. Eventually (in late summer, in temperate climates) along comes a special brood, also to be reared carefully by bee or wasp elder sisters. These new females will be privileged to become layers of eggs, and the males (in bees, called drones) will have only one duty to perform in their entire short lives. This is to fertilize the eggs of the aspiring queens on wedding flights. Many males will never mate, however, and few of the young queens will survive the perils of nature that confront them to start queendoms of their own.

Termites (called "white ants," though not closely related to ants, bees, and wasps) also have amazing societies, but with differ-

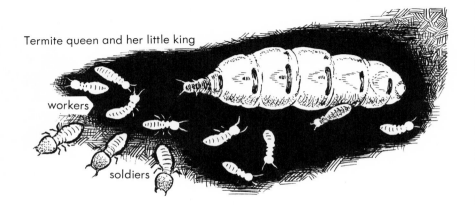

Termite queen and her little king

workers

soldiers

ences. Some of their communities are enormous, numbering their populations in the millions. Certain kinds build extensive tunnels through dry wood, such as beams of old houses or in logs or dead trees, where in dark chambers they, too, care expertly for their eggs and the grubs that hatch from them. Others, more of the tropics, begin their nesting underground but build upward to erect hills or edifices as tall as a man, partially of mud, with almost steel-like hardness and indestructibility. Here at last we find kings! Or at least a prince-consort to each queen—a royal couple who may remain together for years—he small, she with immensely enlarged abdomen filled with huge quantities of eggs. She will lay great numbers of them daily. Here in termite communes and supercities, unlike our other three insect societies, male workers share tasks beside their sisters, though here also neither will reproduce. Only at long intervals will there hatch mating sexes that fly off to try to begin colonies elsewhere.

Within each of these four groups is an interweaving of relationships and communication, much of the latter being by means of odors and chemicals. All four insects have survived many millions of years, from long before there were any mammals on this planet. It is entirely possible they will be flourishing long after human beings have departed from the earth. What is the secret of success of the Siphonophores and the social insects?

If these jellyfish had a motto it would surely be, "One for all and all *are* one." Each submember has become so specialized it is utterly needful of its teammates, the other zooids of the colony, and it blends into its neighbors enough to almost lose its identity as an individual.

Social insects, as we have seen, are only a step less dependent, in that their members are not physically adjoined to one another. But each one, like Siphonophore zooids, is really just a part of a body. Here, also, their specialization of structure, plus the devoted care of eggs and immatures, spell the survival of the community. The good of the whole group, especially of new generations, comes before the comfort of any worker-member, in fact, before their lives. Ants, apparently without fear for themselves, in times of danger have no instinct but to preserve their commune's precious eggs and grublike larvae, rushing them to places of greater safety. A traveling or fleeing colony will cling tenaciously together to form a curious vine that drifts across a stream, anchored at one end to something solid, over which nurses carry their charges. In times of flood or bad weather workers may ball up in a tight cluster with eggs, larvae, and queen at its center, and float away or wait out the disaster. Honey bees, which sting a creature they believe to be a threat in the vicinity of the hive, usually lose their lives when the stinger is torn from them. Termite soldiers have the sole duty of positioning themselves in the path of danger, while more helpless workers and young rush to the protective, innermost regions of their passageways.

Workers of all these insects have no lives of personal "fulfillment," even of much eating or resting. Indeed, in all but termites, it is their diets inadequate in certain nutrients that largely keep them sterile. Most wear themselves out with heavy labor. Many queens themselves become little more than egg-laying machines. Such caste members are but cogs in a committee.

These ancient societies could well laugh, if they were able, at the lesser efficiency of earth's later-arriving birds and mammals. But for all their survival powers, something is lacking in them. Obviously, no zooid or social insect has "a mind of its own," or any "rights" in its group. The wolf, blue jay, and baboon have something of individuality; no two are exactly alike. In spite of rules and regulations that must govern its behavior, each can, for better or worse, go off in its own direction if it takes a notion. Such individuals may pay a penalty for their greater independence —they may gain or fail by their actions—but they still possess some capacity to exert their own will, for they are less controlled by innate patterns.

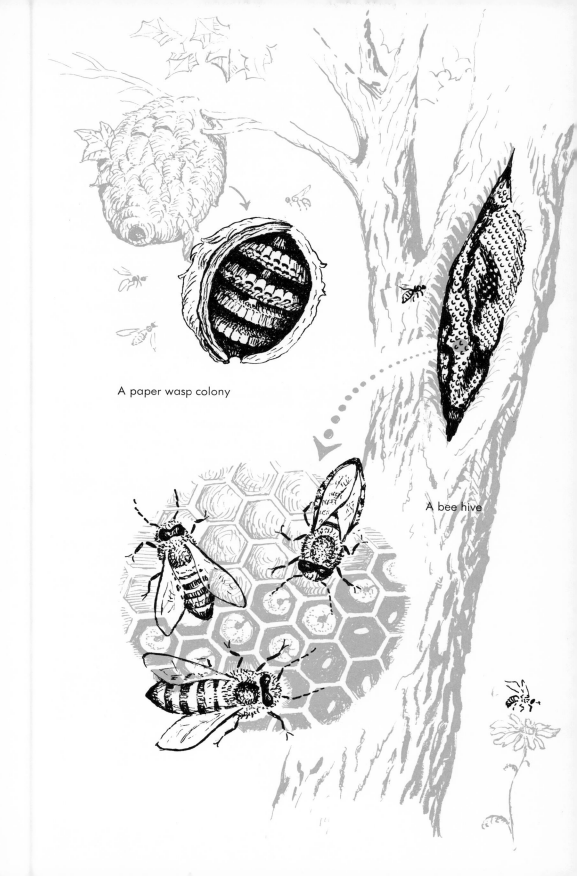

A paper wasp colony

A bee hive

Social insects are selfless; higher vertebrates could be said to be more selfish. Nevertheless, vertebrates also care devotedly for their offspring, sometimes fight valiantly for their group, or stay by the side of a downed comrade. But self-sacrifice is not a programmed part of their behavior as much as it is with social insects. Courage and heroism exist among feathered and furry creatures, and more so among the two-legged and furless mammals. The higher that animal life moves up the scale of development, the more does concern for others become a matter of personal choice, and true nobility.

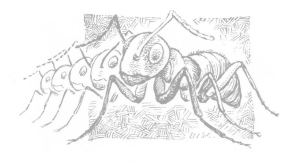

Epilogue: A Word About Human Beings

THIS IS A BOOK about animals, not people. But human beings are a species of animal, and the more we study those kinds less advanced than we are, the more do certain simililarities and contrasts between their behavior and ours spring to attention. Though we are far from knowing all the answers, we cannot help but ask many questions. Here are a few:

    —Is there a basic need in people for belonging to some group(s), and if so, why? What place is there for loners and "the different ones" of the world?

    —In a truly democratic society, should there be rank orders or should everyone be of equal level in importance and authority?

    —Can we draw conclusions for human groups regarding the disadvantageous behavior that often results from overcrowding in animal groups?

    —Can we draw any conclusions about human male or female differences or superiority from studying various societies of animals, and observing their sex roles and leadership?

    —It has been found that human warfare often depends more on loyalty to a group or to leaders than on actual hatred of an enemy. In that case, what should be done about organized killing? Or is it necessary to blame human aggression on some probably nonexistent instinct, and "blow off steam" through continued violence?

—Is complete freedom for everyone an advantage or disadvantage, and is it a fundamental right? If the latter is true, do other animals have rights also?

—Which right comes first, "mine" or "yours"? In other words, does a person owe his first obligation to himself or to his society?

—Are the comparisons we notice between the behavior of human beings and "the beasts" a matter of coincidence, or are they due to any extent to a closer kinship as we go our ways, alone and together?

Suggested Reading

Armstrong, E. A. *The Way Birds Live*. New York: Dover Publications, 1967.

Berrill, Jacquelyn. *Wonders of the World of Wolves*. New York: Dodd, Mead & Company, 1970.

Brown, Leslie. *The Mystery of the Flamingoes*. London: Country Life, 1959.

Buyukmihci, Hope Sawyer. *Hour of the Beaver*. New York: Rand, McNally & Co., 1971.

Caras, Roger. *North American Mammals*. New York: Meredith Press, 1967.

Carrighar, Sally. *The Twilight Seas*. New York: Weybright & Talley, 1975.

Costello, David. *The World of the Prairie Dog*. New York: J. B. Lippincott Company, 1970.

Crisler, Lois. *Arctic Wild*. New York: Harper & Row, 1958 and 1973.

Douglas-Hamilton, Iain and Oria. *Among the Elephants*. New York: The Viking Press, 1975.

George, Jean Craighead. *Julie of the Wolves*. New York: Harper & Row, 1972.

Gilbert, Bil. *The Weasels*. New York: Pantheon Books, 1970.

Hutchins, Ross. *The Ant Realm*. New York: Dodd, Mead & Co., 1967.

MacKinnon, John. *In Search of the Red Ape*. New York: Holt, Rinehart & Winston, 1974.

Ryden, Hope. *God's Dog*. New York: Coward, McCann & Geoghagan, 1975.

————. *Mustangs: A Return to the Wild*. New York: The Viking Press, 1972.

Schlein, Miriam. *Giraffe: The Silent Giant*. New York: Four Winds Press, 1976.

Simon, Hilda. *Exploring the World of Social Insects*. New York: Vanguard Press, 1962.

Thomas, Harold. *Coyotes—Last Animals on Earth?* New York: Lothrop, Lee & Shepard, 1975.

Periodicals:

Animal Kingdom. New York Zoological Society, Bronx, New York 10460.

Defenders of Wildlife. 1244 Nineteenth Street, N.W., Washington, D.C. 20036.

National Wildlife. 1412 16th Street N.W., Washington, D.C. 20036.

Index

African wild dog, 37, 54, 58, 68-69
Aggregation, 11, 84
Aggression, 27, 46, 53-56
Altruism, 87
Antelopes, 12, 24, 26, 33
Ants, 39, 111-114, 116
Apes, 13, 15, 20, 90-100
"Aunties," 13, 28, 85, 87, 112

Baboons, 14, 23, 30, 39, 93, 95-97, 107, 116
Bachelors, 14, 26, 75, 80, 87, 91, 96
Bears, 12, 19, 20, 21, 22, 25, 27, 32, 34, 36, 55, 58, 101, 102-105
Beaver, 13, 35
Bees, 15, 111, 114, 115, 116, 117
Bighorn sheep, 18, 21, 55, 72, 73, 79
Birds, 12, 18, 19, 21, 23, 24, 25, 26, 28, 31, 32, 41-52, 54, 106
Bison, 58
Blue jay, 51, 116
Boa constrictor, 95
Bobcat, 27, 103, 104, 105
Bond, companionship, 30
    mother-young, 28, 85
    pair, 25, 26, 27, 41, 43, 44, 89
Booby, blue-footed, 49
Bowerbird, satin, 49
Bushbaby, 92, 93, 94
Butterflies, 18, 111

Canada lynx, 39
Cape hunting dog, 68-69
Cardinals, 42
Caribou, 18, 72
Carnivores, 21, 65, 66, 67, 71, 72
Cat, pet, 25, 33, 39, 69
Cheetah, 95, 102, 103
Chimpanzee, 40, 90, 92, 93, 94, 98, 106
Colony, 16, 47, 110, 112, 113, 115
Communication, 28, 29, 37, 39, 40, 47, 54, 77
Companionship bond, 30
Cougar, 31, 103
Courtship, 25, 44, 47, 48, 49, 50
Coyote, 12, 32, 45, 59, 64, 102, 105
Crabs, 17, 35, 39
Cranes, 43
Crocodiles, 34

Darling, Sir Frank Fraser, 74-76
Deer, 12, 34, 35, 55, 75, 77-78
Diurnal animals, 23
Dog, pet, 7, 25
Dolphin, 84, 85, 86
Dominance hierarchy, 36, 37, 67
Dragonflies, 34
Ducks, wild, 42, 49

Eagle, 21, 44
Elephants, 13, 15, 20, 28, 85-87, 88, 99, 104

Elk, 35, 73, 74, 107
Estrus, 25, 92
Ethologists, 20, 63, 71, 107

Families, 12, 13, 42, 43, 45, 48, 84, 91, 94
Fighting, 53-56
Fish, 12, 18, 19, 20, 23, 32, 39, 54
Flamingoes, 46
Fox, 12, 35, 59, 64, 99
Frogs, 19, 20, 24, 34

Geese, wild, 44, 51
Gibbon, 13, 15, 91, 92, 93, 99
Giraffe, 58, 89
Gorilla, 20, 31, 36, 37, 90, 92, 93, 97, 98, 107
Grazers, 21, 23
Grooming, 38, 39, 78, 97, 100
Gulls, 14, 17, 47

Harem, 14, 75, 76, 77, 78, 79, 91, 93
Hawk, 44, 45, 57, 59, 61
"Heat, in," 25
Helper-birds, 46
Herbivores, 21, 65, 72
Herds, 21, 23, 72-76, 84, 87, 103, 107, 113
Herring gull, 47-48
Hippopotamus, 35, 89, 99
Howler monkeys, 55, 92, 93
Human beings, 31, 33, 40, 53, 56, 57, 59, 61, 113, 119-120
Hummingbird, 42
Hyenas, 34, 54, 66-68, 69, 70

Innate behavior, 32, 33-35
Insects, 24, 31, 110-117
Instinct, 32, 33, 57

Jackal, 12, 64
Jaguar, 58, 102, 103
Jellyfish, 17, 110, 111, 113, 115

Killing, 55, 56-61
Kob, Uganda, 26, 45
Kuo, Dr. Z. Y., 33

Ladybird beetles, 20
Langur monkeys, 92
Leadership, 12, 51, 67, 69, 73, 75, 76, 92
Learning, 32, 33, 57
Lemmings, 18
Lemur, mouse, 91, 93
Leopard, 19, 22, 95, 102
Lion, 14, 39, 54, 69, 70, 71, 102, 107
Lizard, 19, 31, 34, 39, 54
Locust, 18
Lynx, Canada, 103

Man, 56, 58, 59, 90
Matriarch, 15, 78, 79
Matriarchies, 15, 76
Mice, 19, 20, 59
Migration, 16, 17, 51
Mockingbird, 43
Monkeys, 7, 13, 15, 32, 55, 90-100
Moose, 35, 59, 74
Mother-young bond, 28, 85
Moths, 10
Mountain lion, 31, 79, 102
Mustangs, 79, 80

Nocturnal animals, 93, 104
Nomads, 11, 20, 104, 107
Nurseries, 46, 74, 112

Octopus, 39
Omnivore, 20
Opossum, 105
Orangutan, 34, 91, 93, 103
Ostrich, 42
Ovum, 19, 25, 27
Owl, 41

124

Packs, 13, 59, 63-69, 84, 107
Painted snipe, 42
Pair bond, 25, 26, 27, 41, 43, 44, 89
Peacock, 49
Pecking order, 37
Penguins, 13, 17, 42, 44, 46
Phalarope, 43, 49
Pigeon, 49
Play, 105, 106
Porcupine, 22, 25, 105, 106
Portuguese man-of-war, 110
Potto, 91, 93, 94
Prairie chicken, 44
Prairie dog, 24, 36, 59
Predators, 21, 22, 23, 47, 56-60, 61, 63-71, 96
Prey, 22, 24, 59, 60, 66, 71
Primates, 90-100
Pronghorn, 14, 33
Puma, 8, 31, 33, 35, 102
Python, 95

Rabbits, 19, 24, 35, 53, 59
Raccoon, 105
Rank order, 36, 65, 67
Raptors, 47
Rats, 33, 47, 59
Red deer, 74-76
Reindeer, 76
Rhea, 42
Rhinoceros, 89
Robin, 27, 41, 49
Roe deer, 12

Sage grouse, 26, 43, 44
Sea birds, 16, 46, 47
Sea otter, 27
Seals, 16, 18
Serval, 103
Sex, 19, 20, 24, 25
Siphonophores, 110, 113, 114
Skunk, 22, 105
Snakes, 24

Society, definition, 9
Solitaries, 10, 24, 30, 51, 85, 87, 91, 94, 102-107, 109
Solitary wasp, 117
Spacing, 33-35, 42, 54
Sparrow, 49
Starlings, 23

Termites, 111, 114-116
Territory, 27, 42, 47, 48, 51
Tiger, 57, 102, 103, 104
Tinbergen, Dr. Niko, 48
Toads, 12
Troops, 7, 15, 16, 91, 93, 94, 95
Turtle, 32

Uganda kob, 26, 45
"Uncles," 13

Velella, 111

Wapiti, 73
Wart hog, 12, 18
Wasps, 7, 111, 114, 115
Weasel, 58, 59
Whales, 7, 13, 14, 85-87, 88, 101, 106
Whitetail deer, 77
Wild cats, 78, 102, 103, 104, 105, 107
Wild geese, 13, 18, 44
Wild horses, 14, 39, 79, 99
Wild hunting dog, 37, 54, 58, 68-69
Wild mountain goat, 73
Wild mountain sheep, 14, 18, 21, 72, 73
Wildebeests, 58, 70, 72
Wolf, 12, 13, 21, 22, 34, 45, 57, 58, 59, 61, 63-66, 68, 69, 107
Woodchuck, 20, 35, 59, 105, 106
Woodpecker, 43
Wren, 42

Zebras, 14, 23, 39, 70, 78, 79, 101
Zooids, 110, 111

MARGARET COSGROVE, originally a medical artist, chose to study the broader fields of animals and their interrelationships. Feeling that the study of anatomy and structure is meaningless without an understanding of the total living organism, her recent books have grown out of her deep interest in animal behavior. She wrote on the communication of animals in *Messages and Voices*, which was selected as an Outstanding Science Trade Book for Children. Now, in *Animals Alone and Together*, she explores their social behavior. Her *Bone for Bone*, a stimulating introduction to comparative anatomy, was an ALA Notable Children's Book.

Miss Cosgrove has also written a number of books for younger children, including *Wintertime for Animals, Plants in Time*, and *Seeds, Embryos, and Sex*. She enjoys keeping in direct touch with the world of her readers by teaching art at The Spence School in New York City.